Removing suckers.

Protection for the winter.

The author
Gerhard Worm studied
gardening at the technical
college for gardening in Berlin-
Dahlem. Since 1983 he has
worked as a gardening and
plant advisor on the island of
Mainau where he is responsible
for environmental protection
and organic gardening and
where he runs specialist
seminars on natural issues.

The photographer
Jürgen Becker studied art and
film making. For the last
fourteen years he has worked
as a freelance photographer for
several well-known book and
calendar publishers as well as
for international periodicals and
magazines. The main focus of
his work is on garden, plant,
architectural and landscape
photography.

The illustrator
György Jankovics trained as a
graphic artist at the art
academies of Budapest and
Hamburg. He has produced
illustrations of animals and
plants for a number of well-
known publishing companies
and has also illustrated many
titles in the "Success with ..."
series.

NB: Please read the Author's
notes on page 61 so that your
enjoyment of rose gardening
may remain unimpaired.

A garden full of roses

Whether they contribute grace, elegance or sheer baroque exuberance, roses seem to cast a spell on both small and large gardens. Providing you plant the right variety in the right position, rose care can be problem-free. The following pages will tell you all you need to know about successful rose growing.

Above: The wonderfully scented Remontant rose "Roger Lambelin" has dark red flowers.
Left: The climbing rose "Bobbie James" throws a splendid white mantle of flowers over the walls of this house.

A garden full of roses

Roses in the garden

Because they come in so many shapes and varieties, roses offer many different possibilities for design in your garden. They can stand individually as solitary plants, be grouped in beds, cover a bank or climb up a housewall or over a pergola.

Species roses

These roses, which usually have single, five-petalled flowers, developed entirely in the wild. Nearly all species roses flower only once a year but also bear attractive hips in the autumn.
In a garden: Species roses will creep or climb and can be grown as bushes. They can be used for hedges and fences, for creating greenery and to anchor the soil on slopes or verges. Even the smallest garden usually has some space for a seat surrounded by climbing roses.

Shrub roses

Their dimensions are very similar to those of wild and ornamental bushes. They will often grow taller than 2 m (80 in), may possess single or double flowers and may flower once, several times or continuously. Shrub roses include modern varieties, old roses and English roses.
In the garden: Shrub roses look good either free-standing or in small groups. Small varieties planted as a hedge will provide a visual screen and shelter for wildlife.

Climbing roses

The varieties are differentiated according to their flowers and shape of growth.
● Climbers have stiff, upright shoots. They will climb up to 6 m (20 ft) without support. The flowers, which grow in clusters, and often have large individual blooms, will appear only once or throughout the summer season depending on the variety.
● Rambling roses have thin or soft, creeping or hanging shoots. They will require support to grow upwards. With very few exceptions, they have small flowers which appear in clusters once a year.
In the garden: Climbing roses can be grown on rose arches, fences and espaliers, up walls and over pergolas. They are well suited to small gardens.

Bedding roses

This group includes large-flowered roses and those that produce clusters of flowers several times in succession from the main flowering time in the first month of summer to the first frosts.

● Hybrid tea roses have large flowers, nearly always double, on long stalks.
In the garden: They are most attractive in small groups grown in borders or in classic rose beds.
● Polyantha roses bear many flowers on the end of one stalk. They appear in several umbels or panicles and as single or double varieties.
In the garden: They are suitable for larger areas but will also create an attractive focal point if set in small groups. Good for combining with herbaceous perennials and summer flowers.
● Floribunda roses were created by crossing hybrid tea roses with Polyantha roses. They occur as both single or double flowers and in clusters of different sizes.
In the garden: They are easy to combine with colourful perennials, but also look good in small groups. Individual varieties are suitable for groundcover or for hedges.
● Miniature roses may grow to 30 cm (12 in) tall and will spread out in a broad fan or in a loose, more upright shape. They generally flower several times and bear many small flowers in clusters.
In the garden: They require a position where they can dominate the space available and will receive plenty of sun. Dainty cushion-forming perennials are the ideal partners for them.

Groundcover roses

These roses vary greatly with respect to growth, from very low-growing, sometimes growing vigorously, to low-arching or overhanging sprays or a taller, more upright bush (up to 2 m/80 in). They have simple to very double flowers and bloom in clusters, once or several times.
In the garden: They will cover the ground so thickly that weeds will not stand a chance. These very disease-resistant roses will grow well in a border or on the slope beside a patio. They are good for combining with woody perennials and summer annuals.

Standards and cascades

These grafted rose varieties flower on the stocks of 60-140 cm (24-56 in) tall species roses.
● Standard roses are grown on the stocks of large-flowered varieties or those that produce flowers in clusters.
In the garden: They are most effective as individual plants. Underplanted with summer flowers, perennials or groundcover roses, they will provide an eye-catching spectacle even in a small garden.
● Cascade roses are climbing roses, usually ramblers, which have been grafted on to stocks.
In the garden: Their garlands of flowers will grow profusely and decoratively.

The structure of a rose

The rose (genus name *Rosa*) belongs to the plant family *Rosaceae*.
The root
● Roses with genuine rose roots (species roses or varieties grown from seed) possess a rootstock (a) with strong main roots growing deep into the soil and a widespread net of lateral roots.
● Grafted roses, which grow on a genetically different root (species stock), will having a grafting point (b) above the neck of the root; propagation takes place here through grafting.
The main stem consists of
● several years' worth of woody lateral shoots (e);
● one-year-old shoots (g);
● newly emerged axil shoots, the "eyes" or buds (d) that are situated between the shoot and the leaf stalk;
● dormant buds (c) that normally do not shoot;
● suckers (f) that grow out of the stock below the grafting point and have to be cut off (see pp. 26 and 32);
● single, feathery leaves (h);
● thorns (k) that lie on top of the bark and are easy to break off without seriously damaging the bark;
● flowers (i) – in addition to single flowering roses (five to eight petals), there are semi-double ones (with up to twenty petals), double and very double flowering ones (with more than 70 petals). The flower shape varies from urn-shaped to pompon, globular, ball-shaped and quartered. Roses flower once or several times;
● rosehips (j) are the fruits of the species roses, which differ in shape and colour.

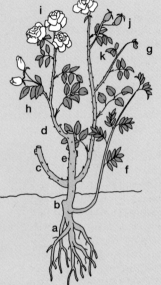

A garden full of roses

Species roses: Those species of roses that developed in the wild are the ancestors of all the varieties. Their natural area of occurrence stretches from the temperate to subtropical climatic zones of the northern hemisphere. Our indigenous species roses are naturally hardy and have adapted well to our soil and climatic conditions. European roses (see p. 10: *Rosa foetida, Rosa hugonis, Rosa moyesii*) are distinguished by their hardiness and simple requirements as to care.

Climbing roses: Their natural predecessors are species roses that creep along the ground, such as *Rosa wichuraiana*, which arrived in Germany from China in 1861, and those that grow through trees and bushes, like *Rosa multiflora*, for example, of which the variety "Carnea" was introduced to Britain from eastern Asia in 1804. From 1940 onwards the cultivars created by Wilhelm Kordes opened up completely new possibilities with respect to hardiness, robustness and willingness to flower.

"Rose de Resht"

Rosa canina

"New Dawn"

"Königin von Danemark"

"Rosarium Uetersen"

"Freisinger Morgenrote"

"Flammentanz"

"Ilse Krohn Superior"

"Westerland"

"Golden Showers"

Shrub roses: In Europe, up until the eighteenth century, alongside the species roses there were also varieties of Gallica, Damask, Alba and Centifolia roses – all nowadays referred to as the "old roses". They flowered only once a year. From 1750 roses began arriving from China and, by crossing these, raisers created plants that flowered more than once: Portland, Bourbon, Noisette, tea roses and, finally, the Remontant roses that are now looked upon as the link between the old roses and the modern varieties. The English roses, cultivars created by Englishman David Austin, combine the charm of the Old Roses with the advantages of modern varieties. The plant table on pages 10 and 11 offers a selection of robust species, climbing and shrub roses.

Beautiful climbing and shrub roses

A garden full of roses

Species roses

Species	Colour	Flower	Hips	Growth	Remarks
Rosa arvensis	white	small, single	spherical dark red	creeping 100-200 cm (3-7 ft)	Field rose; creeping rose; thin shoots; also climber
Rosa canina	delicate pink to white	medium large, single	oval, 2 cm (1 in) long, orange to scarlet	shrub up to 300 cm (10 ft)	Dog rose; with hook-shaped thorns; climber
Rosa carolina	light pink	medium large, single	flat spherical, bristly red	shrub up to 150 cm (5 ft)	Meadow rose; will also thrive on nutrient-poor soils
Rosa foetida	deep yellow	small, single	spherical, brick red	shrub up to 150 cm (5 ft)	Austrian briar; unpleasant scent; susceptible to disease
Rosa gallica	pink to light red	medium large, single	round, brick red	shrub up to 150 cm (5 ft)	French rose; long underground rhizomes
Rosa hugonis	light yellow	medium large, single	broad spherical, black red	shrub up to 250 cm (8 ft)	Early flowering; hardy in frost and vigorously growing
Rosa moyesii	wine red	medium large, single	bottle shaped, up to 6 cm (2 in) long, orange red	shrub up to 300 cm (10 ft)	Delicate foliage; very attractive as a solitary plant
Rosa pimpinellifolia	white, delicate pink	medium large, single	flat spherical, brown black	shrub up to 100 cm (3 ft)	Scotch rose; delicate scent; will thrive on the poorest soils

Shrub roses

Variety	Raiser	Colour	Flower	Growth	Remarks
"Freisinger Morgenrote"	Kordes 1988	orange, pink edges	large, double	up to 200 cm (7 ft), vigorous growth	Flowers several times; robust; attractive as a solitary plant
"Hansaland"	Kordes 1993	brilliant red	medium large, semi-double	180 cm (6 ft), broad bushy	Flowers several times; ideal for hardy hedges
"Königin von Danemark"	Booth 1816	silvery rose	medium large, fairly double	200 cm (7 ft), overhanging	*Rosa alba*; single flowering; strong scent
"Kordess's Brillant"	Kordes 1983	lobster red	large, loosely double	up to 200 cm (7 ft), bushy	Flowers several times; robust; faint scent
"Roger Lambelin"	Schwartz 1890	carmine red, white edges	large, densely double	150 cm (5 ft), strong, well branched	Remontant rose; flowers several times; crinkled petals; scented
"Madame Isaac Pereire"	Garcon 1881	carmine pinkish-red, with purple	large, fairly double	over 200 cm (7 ft), strong upright	Bourbon rose; flowers several times; also climbing; strong scent
"Muscosa"	Holland 1796	intense pink	medium large, very double	100 cm (3 ft), loose structure	*Rosa centifolia* "Muscosa", moss rose; single flowering; intense scent
"Fritz Nobis"	Kordes 1940	salmon pink	large, loosely double	up to 200 cm (7 ft), broad bushy	Single flowering; wavy petal edges; strong scent
"Pink Robusta"	Kordes 1986	brilliant pure pink	medium large, semi-double	up to 200 cm (7 ft), very branching	Flowers several times; hardy; good visual screen
"Rose de Resht"	from Iran	fuchsia pink	small, very double	up to 150 cm (5 ft), upright, robust	Damask rose; flowers often; hardy
"Rosenresli"	Kordes 1982	orange pink to carmine red	medium large, fairly double	up to 150 cm (5 ft), broad bushy	Flowers often; recommended; strong scent
"Schneewittchen"	Kordes 1958	pure snow white	medium large, fairly double	up to 150 cm (5 ft), bushy, upright	Flowers often; shoots hang in arcs; robust
"Westerland"	Kordes 1969	glowing copper orange	large, loosely double	up to 200 cm (7 ft), broad bushy	Flowers often; recommended; robust

Climbing roses

Variety	Raiser	Colour	Flower	Growth	Remarks
"Albertine"	Barbier 1921	copper pink to salmon pink	medium large, loosely double	shoots up to 400 cm (13 ft), lots of thorns	Rambler; flowers once; healthy foliage; strong scent
"Alchymist"	Kordes 1956	orange yellow	large, fully double	strong shoots, up to 200 cm (7 ft)	Climber; flowers once; healthy foliage; robust
"Bobbie James"	Sunningdale Nurseries 1961	creamy white	small, single, bowl shaped	very vigorous growth, over 500 cm (17 ft)	Rambler; flowers once; dark red hips
"Compassion"	Harkness 1974	salmon pink, orange tints	large, very double	up to 200 cm (7 ft), stiffly upright	Climber; flowers often; robust; hardy
"Coral Dawn"	Boerner-Jackson & Perkins 1952	coral pink	large, loosely double	up to 300 cm (10 ft), vigorous climber	Climber; continuous flowering; abundant flowers; robust
"Felicite et Perpetue".	Jacques 1827	white, breath of pink	small, densely double rosette-like	strong, overhanging, up to 500 cm (17 ft)	Rambler; flowers once; attractive as cascade rose
"Flammentanz"	Kordes 1955	blood red	medium large, fully double	very stiff, up to 400 cm (13 ft)	Climber; flowers once; hardy; freestanding position
"Goldener Olymp"	Kordes 1984	golden yellow	large, fully double	over 200 cm (7 ft), bushy branching	Climber; flowers often; robust; hardy
"Golden Showers"	Germain's Seed & Plant Co. 1958	lemon yellow	large, double	up to 300 cm (10 ft), upright to bushy	Climber; flowers once; good visual screen on pergola
"Guinee"	Mallerin 1938	dark red	large, fully double	strong shoots, up to 400 cm (13 ft)	Climber; flowers once; beautiful yellow filaments
"Harlekin"	Kordes 1986	creamy white, red edges	large, extremely double	up to 250 cm (8 ft), bushy	Climber; flowers often; strong scent
"Ilse Krohn Superior"	Kordes 1964	brilliant pure white	large, double	up to 300 cm (10 ft), bushy, vigorous growth	Climber; flowers often; robust; very hardy
"New Dawn"	Somerset Nursery 1930	delicate whitish-pink	medium large, extremely double	up to 300 cm (10 ft), spreading arcs	Climber; flowers often; hardy; robust; scented
"Paul's Scarlet Climber"	Paul 1915	carmine red	large, semi-double	bushy, shoots to 300 cm (10 ft)	Climber; flowers once; robust; not on south-facing site
"Raubritter"	Kordes 1936	light purple pink	small, ball shaped, double	densely bushy, up to 300 cm (10 ft), vigorous growth	Rambler; flowers once; attractive cascade rose
"Rosarium Uetersen"	Kordes 1977	dark pink	very large, very double	densely bushy, up to 200 cm (7 ft)	Climber; flowers often; robust; particularly hardy
"Santana"	Tantau 1985	dark blood red	large, double	up to 200 cm (7 ft), bushy, upright	Climber; flowers often; robust; hardy
"Schwanensee"	McGredy 1968	brilliant pure white	large, double	stiffly upright, up to 300 cm (10 ft)	Climber; flowers often; slightly scented
"Solo"	Tantau 1956	velvety red	large, loosely double	vigorous growth, shoots about 300 cm (10 ft)	Climber; flowers often; healthy foliage; slightly scented
"Sorbet"	Meilland 1993	delicate pink	large, fully double	bushy, up to 200 cm (7 ft)	Climber; flowers often; resistant
"Super Dorothy"	Hetzel 1986	pure pink	small, fully double	vigorous growth, up to 300 cm (10 ft)	Rambler; flowers often into the autumn; very healthy
"Sympathie"	Kordes 1964	velvety dark red	large, fully double	up to 400 cm (13 ft), vigorous growth	Climber; flowers often; robust; rain resistant
"Veilchenblau"	Schmidt 1909	purple violet, white centre	small, single or semi-double	vigorous growth, up to 400 cm (13 ft)	Rambler; flowers once; hardy; very healthy foliage

A garden full of roses

Grafted roses first became available in 1867, when the French raiser Guillot crossed a Remontant rose with a tea rose from China. "La France" was the first tea rose to be put on the market. It has large, double, scented flowers which grow singly on long stems. Many of the following cultivars, however, devloped a susceptibility to black spot and it was not until 1945 that raiser Meilland made the breakthrough to healthy roses with his yellow hybrid tea rose "Gloria Dei".

Polyantha roses were first cultivated in France in 1875 when the raiser Guillot introduced a Polyantha rose to the market, named "Paquerette". Its distinguishing characteristics were large clusters of flowers with relatively small individual flowerheads.

Floribunda roses: About 50 years later, Danish raiser Svend Poulsen created his first Floribunda by crossing Polyantha roses with hybrid tea roses. This resulted in frost-hardier varieties which flower abundantly.

"Papa Meilland"

"Flamingo"

"Sutter's Gold"

"Mainaufeuer"

"Betty Prior"

"Helga"

"Pink Meidiland"

Groundcover roses:
This group now includes all roses that cover the ground so densely that weeds cannot grow. Among them are prostrate, creeping varieties like the climbing rose "Max Graf" and also various taller varieties like the Polyantha "The Fairy" or the shrub rose "Palmengarten Frankfurt".
The plant table on pages 14 and 15 offers a selection of robust bedding and groundcover roses.

"Queen Elizabeth"

Beautiful bedding and groundcover roses

"Eden Rose"

"Friesia"

A garden full of roses

Bedding roses: hybrid tea roses

Variety	Raiser	Colour	Flower	Growth	Remarks
"Aachener Dom"	Meilland 1982	light salmon pink	large, very double	60-80 cm (24-32 in), bushy, vigorous	Recommended rose; scented; very healthy
"Beaute"	Mallerin 1953	golden orange	very large, loosely double	60 cm (24 in), vigorous, bushy	Luxuriant foliage; slightly scented
"Crimson Glory"	Kordes 1935	velvet red	medium large, fairly double	60 cm (24 in), spreading bushy compact	Continuous flowering; wonderful scent
"Duftwolke"	Tantau 1963	orange red, later purple red	very large, fairly double	60 cm (24 in), well branching bushy compact	Recommended rose; large leathery leaves; intense scent
"Duftzauber 84"	Kordes 1984	dark red	large, very double	90 cm (36 in), upright vigorously branching	Flowers often; good scent; robust and hardy
"Eden Rose"	Meilland 1950	strong pink, darker veined	medium large, fairly double	80 cm (32 in), strong, less branching	Strong scent; healthy; shiny green leaves
"Flamingo"	Kordes 1979	delicate pink	medium large, fairly double	80 cm (32 in), luxuriant growth, bushy	Flowers often; robust; good cut flower
"Gloria Dei"	Meilland 1945	light yellow with pink edges	very large, densely double	100 cm (40 in) tall, bushy	Continuous flowering; very hardy slightly scented
"Josphine Baker"	Meilland 1973	dark red	medium large, densely double	80 cm (32 in), strong, upright	Elegant; single flowers on long stems; flowers well
"King's Ransom"	Morey-Jackson & Perkins 1961	golden yellow, darker veins	very large, fairly double	90 cm (36 in), vigorous growth	Continuous flowering; strongly scented; tough, shiny foliage
"Kleopatra"	Kordes 1994	wine red inside old gold on outside	medium large, fairly double	60 cm (24 in), bushy	Flowers well; scented; robust; healthy foliage
"Papa Meilland"	Meilland 1963	dark red	medium large, fairly double	80 cm (32 in), evenly bushy	Olive green, shiny foliage; strong scent
"Schwarze Madonna"	Kordes 1992	velvety black red	large, densely double	60-80 cm (24-32 in), plenty of shoots, much branching	Elegant shape; shiny foliage; good for cut flowers
"Sutter's Gold"	Swim/Arm-strong 1950	orange yellow, reddish glow	medium large, fairly double	80 cm (32 in), stiffly upright, branching	Abundant flowers; narrow, shiny leaves; strong scent

Bedding roses: Polyantha and Floribunda roses

Variety	Raiser	Colour	Flower	Growth	Remarks
"Allgold"	Le Grice 1957	glowing golden yellow	medium large, semi-double	40 cm (16 in), broad bushy	Abundantly flowering; rain resistant
"Bella Rosa"	Kordes 1982	vigorous pink	medium large, densely double	60 cm (24 in), broad bushy, medium strong	Continuous flowering; scented; robust and rain resistant
"Betty Prior"	Prior & Sons 1935	carmine pink, lighter inside	medium large, single	80 cm (32 in), stiffly upright, bushy	Continuous flowering; will stand semi-shade; very hardy
"Europeana"	de Ruiter 1964	carmine red	medium large, rosette-like double	70 cm (28 in), loosely upright	Continuous flowering; also suitable for larger beds
"Friesia"	Kordes 1973	glowing golden yellow	large, loosely double	60 cm (24 in), upright, well branching	Recommended; delicious scent; rain resistant; frost hardy
"Gartenzauber 84"	Kordes 1984	glowing blood red	very large, densely double	60 cm (24 in), upright, well branching	Beautiful shape; flowers often; rain resistant; slight scent
"Helga"	de Ruiter 1975	pure white	large, double	60-80 cm (24-32 in), upright, strong	Abundantly flowering; light green shiny foliage

Bedding and groundcover roses

Variety	Raiser	Colour	Flower	Growth	Remarks
"Lilli Marleen"	Kordes 1959	velvet dark red	large, loosely double	40 cm (16 in), bushy, strong shoots	Continuous flowering; slight scent; requires regular care
"Mariandel"	Kordes 1985	glowing dark red	medium large, double	60 cm (24 in), compact bushy, upright	Abundantly flowering; slight scent; very robust and hardy
"Muttertag"	Grootendorst 1950	light red	small, loosely double	40 cm (16 in), bushy, upright	Ball-shaped flowers; for roof gardens
"Nina Weibull"	Poulsen 1961	red orange	medium large, densely double	50 cm (20 in), broad bushy, upright	Shiny, leathery foliage; very hardy, robust
"Sarabande"	Meilland 1957	geranium red	medium large, single to slightly double	50 cm (20 in), broad bushy	Luxuriant flowers until first frost; weather resistant
"Shocking Blue"	Kordes 1974	magenta	large, semi-double	60 cm (24 in), bushy, strong	Strongly scented; longlasting cut flowers
"Queen Elizabeth"	Germain's Seed & Plant Co. 1955	delicate light pink	large, loosely double	130 cm (52 in), stiffly upright	Continuous flowering; robust; will stand semi-shade
"Tip Top"	Tantau 1963	salmon pink	large, semi-double	40 cm (16 in), bushy, stunted	Slight scent; sensitive to black spot
"Traumerei"	Kordes 1974	salmon orange	medium large, fully double	70 cm (28 in), broad bushy, strong	Abundantly flowering; intense scent; robust

Groundcover roses

Variety	Raiser	Colour	Flower	Growth	Remarks
"Heidekind"	Kordes 1985	cherry red	medium large, double	80 cm (32 in), bushy, slightly overhanging	Flowers often; decorative dark green foliage; robust
"Heideroslein Nozomi"	Onodera 1968	mother of pearl pink	very small, single	up to 30 cm (12 in), creeping, flat	Flowers once with abundant flowers; robust; frost hardy
"Mainaufeuer"	Kordes 1990	blood red	medium large, double	50 cm (20 in), broad growth	Flowers right through to first frost; shiny foliage; robust
"Max Graf"	Bowditch 1919	glowing pink	medium large, single	50 cm (20 in), low arching	Flowers once; very thorny; completely hardy
"Palmengarten Frankfurt"	Kordes 1988	strong pink	medium large, double	70-100 cm (28-40 in), broadly spreading	Flowers often; very robust; easy to care for
"Rote Max Graf"	Kordes 1980	glowing, velvety red	medium large, single	60 cm (24 in), shoots lie low to 200 cm (80 in)	Flowers once; forms thick cushion; frost hardy
"Royal Bassino"	Kordes 1991	glowing blood red	large, semi-double	60 cm (24 in), broad bushy	Flowers often; glowing colour; shiny foliage
"Sea Foam"	Schwartz 1964	brilliant white	medium large, fully double	100 cm (40 in) tall, up to 200 cm (80 in) wide	Flowers often with abundant flowers; winter hardy
"Snow Ballet"	Clayworth 1978	pure white	medium large, densely double	60 cm (24 in), broad bushy, overhanging	Flowers often; light green foliage; dense groundcover
"Snow Carpet"	McGredy 1980	pure white	small, densely double	20 cm (8 in), flat, remains low growing	Flowers often; forms dense cushions; for small areas
"Sommermarchen"	Kordes 1992	strong pink	small, semi-double	50 cm (20 in), broad bushy	Flowers often; robust; very shiny foliage
"Sommerwind"	Kordes 1985	brilliant pure pink	medium large, semi-double	60 cm (24 in), bushy, very branching	Flowers often until the first frost; robust; recommended
"The Fairy"	Bentall 1932	light pink	small, densely double	60 cm (24 in), broad growing	Flowers often; abundant flowers; overhanging shoots; robust

15

A garden full of roses

Buying roses

You will find roses on sale in all sorts of places but you should not purchase them from unsuitable outlets.

● Tree nurseries and specialist rose nurseries will have an extensive selection and will give advice on position and care.

● If you buy from raisers or through mail order, you will usually order through a catalogue or buy direct.

● Nurseries usually have a specially selected range of roses for sale.

● Garden centres, as a rule, have only the best known varieties in their selection.

How they are offered: Roses can be obtained freshly dug up with bare roots, in a container with a large rootstock ball or well packed in bags and cartons (the roots are usually protected from drying out by being packed in peat and soil).

Tips on choosing roses

The intended planting position will, to a great extent, determine your choice.

Is the rose to be a solitary plant or will it stand in a group? Will the colour of the flower go with the surroundings? Will your rose flower once or several times? What type of growth will it have? In addition to these essential criteria, you will also have to consider a few other points.

Roots: They should be healthy and strong so that the rose will be able to grow properly.

Quality: Roses of the finest quality have a well-branching root system and three vigorous shoots, two of which should be growing out of the grafting point; the third may emerge 5 cm (2 in) above that point. This type will adapt faster and develop more quickly than roses which have only two strong shoots emerging from the grafting point.

Shoots: The green shoots should be smooth and plump. Wrinkled indents that appear when pressure is applied with a finger indicate that the plant has dried out.

Planting time

The best planting time for roses with bare roots is from the second to third months of autumn, while the soil still has enough warmth to encourage root formation. The soil should be neither too wet nor frozen (see p. 18). In regions with a harsh climate or heavy, compacted soil, it is better to plant roses in the first to second months of spring. Large container plants can be planted in frost-free ground all year round; the best times are spring and autumn.

Spacing

The various types of growth, heights and shapes of the many different varieties of rose make exact instructions difficult. You must also take into account the shape of the design of the entire planting and its surrounds. The following general rules apply.

Bedding roses
● slow-growing varieties: 30-40 cm (12-16 in) apart (six to eight plants per square metre);
● vigorously growing varieties: 40-60 cm (16-24 in) apart (three to five plants per square metre).

Groundcover roses
● prostrate, slow-growing: 40-60 cm (16-24 in) apart (three to four plants per square metre);
● low, bushy growing: for a thick carpet 40-60 cm (16-24 in) apart (three to four plants per square metre); for a less compact planting 60-80 cm (24-32 in) apart (two plants per square metre);
● tall, upright to slightly overhanging: the planting distance should equal half the height of growth (in the case of varieties that are 1-2 m (3-7 ft) tall, three plants per square metre).

Climbing roses
For growing on walls
● slow-growing varieties: about 2 m (7 ft);
● faster growing varieties: 3-5 m (10-17 ft).

A charming constrast of red and white roses ("Red Coat" and "Schneewittchen") frame a blue garden seat.

Plant only one climbing rose on a pergola or rose arch to ensure good development.

Shrub roses

● The following applies for group or hedge planting: the distance between each two plants should equal half the height of growth, which means that plants with a mature height of 2 m (7 ft) should be spaced 1 m (40 in) apart.

● Individual planting: up to 3 m (10 ft).

Standards and cascades

These plants are most effective in a freestanding, solitary position. When planted in rows, place tall standards about 3m (10 ft) apart; cascades 3-5 m (10-17 ft) apart.

Sweet-scented "Schneewittchen".

Planting

The best time to plant roses is in the autumn, providing the ground is neither too dry nor frosty. If they have come from a cool nursery, they can also be planted up to the end of spring.

Tips on planting

● Roses that are not going to be planted right away should have their roots heeled in the soil in a shady spot. Stand the plant at an angle in a shallow trench and cover it with soil 5-10 cm (2-4 in) above the grafting point, press the roots down and water well.
● Roses that have been delivered in cold weather or in frost should be packed in protective layers and stored for about six days in a frost-free room. Remove the packaging. Heel the roses into frost-free soil outside for a few days, then plant.
● Roses with very dry roots should be covered with soil for 24 hours and watered well.
● Do not plant in soaking wet soil.
● Do not fertilize on the day of planting. This may damage the roots.
● If the soil has a tendency to waterlogging, before you plant the rose insert a 10 cm (4 in) gravel layer into the planting hole to provide drainage.

How to plant
(illustrations 1-4)

If planting in the autumn, stand the roses for at least two hours in a container of water before planting, so that the roots and the grafting point are covered by the water. If planting in the spring, water well and again in about ten hours.
Planting cut: Shorten the roots to about 20 cm (8 in). Damaged roots should be cut back to the healthy wood.
Spring planting: Shorten all the shoots. Cut strong ones back to five buds, weaker ones back to three buds; very weak shoots should be cut back 3 mm above the point of emergence.

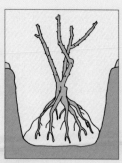

1 Planting a rose: Spread out the roots on a mound of soil.

2 Fill up the planting hole: Press down the soil with your hands.

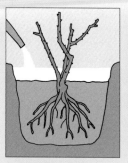

3 Watering: Water up to the edge of the watering gulley.

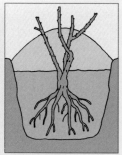

4 Heaping up soil: Heap up soil to a height of 20 cm (8 in).

Digging a planting hole: This should be wide and deep enough for the grafting point to end up 5 cm (2 in) below the surface of the soil and for the roots to be able to spread out loosely in the soil.
Inserting the plant (illustration 1): Mix a little soil with well-rotted compost and heap it up in the middle of the planting hole; set the plant on the heap of soil and spread the roots out.
Filling in the soil (illustration 2): Loosely fill the planting hole with soil. Lift the plant slightly so that the hollow spaces between the roots are filled in. Press the soil down with your hands. This will create a

shallow channel for watering.

Watering (illustration 3): Give the plant enough water to fill the channel to the top. Allow the water to drain away and water again several times.

Filling the plant hole: Once the last lot of water has drained away, fill the channel up with soil. Press down firmly with your hands.

Heaping up soil (illustration 4): Heap good garden soil around the plant to a height of about 20 cm (8 in) as a protection against frost and drying out.

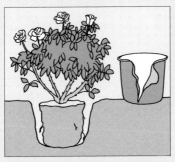

5 Container roses: Remove the rootstock from the pot before planting.

the stake halfway up and again in the lower third of the stake, using sisal rope in a figure of eight. **My tip:** Before tying up, wrap a piece of hessian sacking around the stem under each tie to prevent the rope from rubbing the bark.

Standard roses
(illustration 6)

● Dig the planting hole deep enough so the stem ends up being planted at the same depth as in the tree nursery.
● Push a treated wooden stake firmly into the hole. It should reach to just beneath the beginning of the crown.
● Plant the rose about 10 cm (4 in) from the stake.
● Tie the stem firmly to

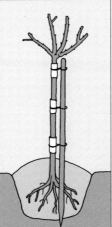

6 Tall standards: Tie the standard to a stake.

Climbing roses
(illustration 7)

Training a rose up a wall espalier.
● Dig the planting hole about 20 cm (8 in) away from the espalier and deep enough for the grafting point to end up 5 cm (2 in) under the soil.
● Position the roots diagonally towards the support in the planting hole.
My tip: Water frequently during the first year so that the roots do not dry out. The housewall will release plenty of heat when the sun is shining on it.
NB: Fasten the espalier to the wall with spacers that create a gap of about 10 cm (4 in) so that the plant is well ventilated and the shoots are easier to tie on.

Container roses
(illustration 5)

Roses grown in plastic pots can be planted all year round.
● Water well before planting.
● Remove the container and set the rose in the soil deep enough for the rootstock and the surface of the soil to be at the same level.
● Fill all hollow spaces with a mixture of soil and compost. Press down.
● Water well. When planting in the summer, water frequently afterwards to prevent the rootstock from drying out.

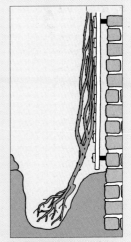

7 Climbing roses lean towards the support.

A garden full of roses

Soil quality

Roses require a loose, deep soil with good drainage (see exhausted soil, p. 23). They thrive best in sandy, permeable soils. Test the soil structure using the finger test.

Soil consistency

● Sandy soils tend to sift easily through one's fingers. They are air- and water-permeable but have a low nutrient content. Adding compost will bind the soil and provide nutrients. In the case of first-time plantings, dig in a 20 cm (8 in) thick layer of humus. For existing rose beds, work compost in loosely and shallowly between the plants every spring.

● Loamy soils crumble between your fingers and will also clump together without being sticky. This medium heavy to heavy, humus-rich soil stores warmth, water, air and nutrients well. To improve permeability, work in a 10 cm (4 in) thick layer of sand.

● In heavy clay soils the soil can be clumped together to form tough lumps. This soil is not easily permeated by water and air, is full of nutrients, warms up slowly and will develop cracks in dry weather. Loosen clay soil by working in sand and compost (ratio 50:50) annually in the spring.

● Marshy soil can be squeezed like a sponge. It is acid, nutrient-poor and contains much water. You will need to add sand, loam, lime and compost. For a first-time planting, improve the soil to a depth of 30-40 cm (12-16 in deep).

Soil preparation: At least three months before planting, dig over the soil to a depth of 60 cm (24 in) with a pick. Loosen the subsoil so that excess water can drain away and will not create waterlogging.

Hoeing: After planting, hoe the ground shallowly every month. This will keep the surface open, improve water circulation and eliminate weeds.

NB: Take care not to injure plant roots when hoeing. Wounds will make the plant more likely to produce suckers.

Mulching

Mulching is covering the soil surface with a thick layer of organic material. This often eliminates the need for hoeing. The mulching layer prevents fast evaporation of moisture through the action of the sun and the wind as well as muddiness after a heavy rainfall. It also prevents weed formation and provides nourishment for soil organisms.

Suitable mulching materials include straw, bark and well-rotted compost. Leaves (but not nut, pear or oak leaves) can only be used if mixed with compost, grass and chopped twigs. Do not use peat.

NB: Only use bark mulch after the roses have established themselves for a year.

How to mulch

● Before mulching, remove tough, resistant weeds like ground elder (*Aegopodium podagraria*).

● Depending on the material used, put down a 4-6 cm (1½-2¼ in) thick layer.

● Once the mulching layer has turned to humus, mix it with the topsoil by loose, shallow hoeing. Then renew the mulch.

The right time to mulch: In late autumn or in the first and second months of spring after pruning and first fertilizing.

The pH value of the soil

The pH value will tell you the degree of acidity of the soil. If the value is around 7 the soil will be neutral; values below 7 characterize an acid soil; values above 7 an alkaline one. The pH value can be determined by using a paper indicator strip which is available in the trade. Roses require a slightly acid, neutral to slightly alkaline soil (pH value between 6.4 and 7.4).

For soils that are too alkaline, add peat or a peat substitute. When planting, mix a third peat and two thirds sandy loam and add this to the planting hole.

For soils that are too acid, add kelp meal or lime in the autumn (read the instructions on dosage given on the packaging).

A magnificent rose arch with climbing rose "Flammentanz".

Watering

As a rule, roses rarely require water as their roots obtain moisture from the deeper layers of the soil.

● Heap up a little wall of soil around the rose so that the water cannot run off into soil further away.

● Freshly planted roses should be watered daily to help them to establish themselves. Older specimens only need watering during long periods of drought.

● Do not pour the water on the flowers and leaves as this will encourage diseases. Water the area around the roots with a slow stream of water.

● Water in the mornings or evenings. Both flowers and leaves will burn if made wet in intense sunlight.

Do not turn on a hosepipe and spray strong jets of water on to the roses as though trying to put out a fire. Use a rose-spray head on the pipe and spray the ground gently like a shower of rain. Make sure that roses under the house eaves, or beside a house wall, are actually receiving water when it rains. Check the soil for moisture.

Replanting roses

Replanting roses should not present any problems as long as you observe a few rules.

Correct replanting

(illustrations 1-5)

Be very careful when replanting healthy old roses.

When to replant:
Replant at the end of the second month of autumn to the first month of winter. In exceptional cases you can also replant in the first and second months of spring.

Pruning: When replanting in the autumn, shorten the shoots slightly and cut out withered wood (exception, see shrub roses). The main pruning should be undertaken in the spring (see p. 30).

The planting hole: Dig the soil over thoroughly in the new position and make the hole deep enough so that the plant ends up at the same level as before.

Placing a cloth around

the rootstock: Wrap a piece of rootstock fabric around the rootball before transporting the plant to its new position.

Lifting the old rose
● Cut a circle with a diameter of 40-60 cm (16-24 in) by making vertical spade thrusts in

the soil under the outer perimeter of the branches (illustration 1).
● Dig away the soil outside this circle. Dig out sections of soil around the rose until you reach the roots which go down deep into the soil (illustration 2). Make sure that as many roots as possible

will remain intact.
● Using diagonal spade thrusts, loosen the rootstock and carefully lift it out (illustration 3).
● Set the plant on the ready prepared fabric and wrap this around the rootstock. This will prevent the soil from falling away from around the roots. You can knot the ends of the fabric around the rootstock or

hold them together with a piece of rope (illustration 4).
● Use a wheelbarrow for transporting heavy rootstocks.
Alternatively, drag the rootstock along the ground on a sheet of thick polythene.
● You can either remove the fabric from

around the rootstock or merely loosen the knot and set the plant, together with the fabric, in the new hole (it will rot away later on). Shovel garden soil in and fill in the gaps at the side.
● Finally, press the soil down firmly with your hands or, very lightly, with a foot. Water the plant well.

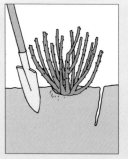

1 Cut out a circle with vertical spade thrusts.

2 Dig out soil all around the plant.

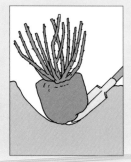

3 Loosen it with diagonal spade thrusts.

4 Wrap the rootstock in fabric and tie it up.

Shrub roses

(illustration 6)

If you want to transplant a very spreading shrub rose in the autumn, cut back the shoots to about 20-30 cm (8-12 in) before digging it up. This will make the job of digging easier and the plant will also be easier to transport to the new position.

Climbing roses

Before transplanting it, the shoots of a climbing rose should be cut back by half. This will ensure that the plant settles well into its new position. Plant as described on page 22, making sure that there will be sufficient room for the plant as it grows and spreads.

5 Set the plant in at the same height as before.

Standard roses

Before replanting, cut the crowns of standards back by about a third.

Soil exhaustion

This may occur if roses have been growing in the same bed for many years. Symptoms include a sudden infestation with disease in spite of adequate soil care, lack of growth and sparse formation of foliage and flowers. New roses that have been planted in an old rose bed may grow weakly if the soil is exhausted.
Causes include unbalanced fertilizing, inadequate nutrients, insufficient ventilation and waterlogging. If old rose stocks are left in the soil, toxic substances may leak from the roots or soil fungi may hinder nutrient extraction by new, young rose plants and thus interfere with their growth. Nematodes (eelworms) may also damage the new plant.
Remedy: Change the position and plant the

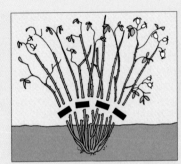

6 Before replanting, shorten the shoots of shrub roses to about three to four buds.

affected roses in fresh soil. Exchange the soil by digging out the old soil to a depth of 60-80 cm (24-32 in) and replacing it with new garden soil.

Replanting gaps in a bed

Occasionally a plant or two will die in your rose bed and you will have to plant new roses in these gaps if you do not want bare patches in the bed.
The right time to plant is in late autumn or in the first to second months of spring.
Choice of plants: The new rose should complement the general colour shades in the bed. The best plan is to choose a plant of the same variety that is already growing around

the gap you intend to fill. The speed at which the new rose will grow must also be considered. If you suddenly plant a fast-growing variety beside slow-growing ones, the growth of the slow-growing ones will be considerably impaired.
Method
● Prune neighbouring roses. This will prevent the accidental breaking off of shoots while you are working around this spot.
● Carefully dig out the old plant.
● Completely remove the old soil in an area of 30 cm (12 in) around to a depth of about 60-80 cm (24-32 in) and replace it with good garden soil.
● Plant the new rose as described on pages 18-19.

A garden full of roses

Plant nutrition

Roses require adequate amounts of nutrients for healthy growth.
The main nutrients
● Nitrogen (N) which influences the growth of shoots and leaves.
● Phosphorus (P) which encourages the formation of flowers and fruit.
● Potassium or potash (K) which regulates the water balance and increases resistance to disease.
● Calcium or lime (Ca) which encourages the formation of roots and shoots and neutralizes acids.
● Magnesium (Mg) which encourages the formation of chlorophyll.
Trace elements, such as iron (Fe), manganese (Mn), zinc (Zn), boron (B), molybdenum (Mo) and copper (Cu) are required in only very small amounts.
By analysing a soil sample you will discover whether the nutrients in your soil are well balanced or not. Some time between autumn and spring (not after fertilizing) use a spade to take soil samples from sixteen different places at a depth of 30 cm (12 in) and a further set of samples at 60 cm (24 in) depth. Mix the samples from the same depths and arrange to send 500 g (1 lb) of each, in sealed plastic bags with labels, to a soil analysis laboratory (ask at your local garden centre for an address). Along with the analysis results, you should also receive advice on fertilizing. You could also buy a soil testing kit and do it yourself.

How fertilizers work

Organic fertilizers contain natural animal and plant matter. Soil organisms gradually transform this into nutrients for plants.
● Dry shredded bark will provide potassium.
● Wood ash (not coal ash!) contains much potassium and magnesium.
● Hoof and horn meal provides nitrogen; a mixture of hoof and horn meal, blood and bonemeal gives nitrogen and phosphorus.
● Dolomite granules, lime and kelp add calcium to the soil (apply as 50-100 g/1½-3 oz per square metre per year).
● Ripe garden compost and well-rotted manure will provide nitrogen.
Mineral fertilizers have been chemically manufactured. The nutrient salts contained in them can be used rapidly by the plant but will endanger soil organisms.
Types of fertilizer
● Multi-nutrient fertilizers can be obtained from the gardening trade as organic, mineral or organo-mineral mixed fertilizers. The nutrient composition (NPK) is usually indicated on the packaging. The ideal mix for roses is 9 per cent nitrogen (N), 6 per cent phosphorus (P) and 12 per cent potassium (K).
● Liquid fertilizers are suitable for alleviating an acute lack of nutrients rapidly and effectively. (Check the correct dosage on the packaging!)

How and when to fertilize

Providing the soil has been adequately prepared, the roses will not need to be fertilized until the first year after planting, when they will have rooted well.
● In dry weather, water the soil well before and after fertilizing so that nutrients can penetrate it.
● Do not sprinkle fertilizers on flowers and leaves. This will cause burns in sunlight.
Use organic fertilizers in late autumn or winter. They take a while to become effective.
● Every year, add 1 kg (2 lb) garden compost per square metre. Every three years add 3 kg (6 lb) of manure per square metre.
● Work in a handful of hoof and horn meal per square metre in the second month of autumn. Another handful can be sprinkled on top of the soil in mid spring.
Use mineral fertilizers in spring when the buds begin to shoot, in the amount of 100-120 g (3½-3 oz) per square metre.
If winter protection has been provided by using manure, reduce the nutrients added in spring by a third. In the first month of summer, after the first flowers have appeared, fertilize again. At the beginning of the first month of autumn, add about 40 g (about 1 oz) potassium fertilizer per square metre to encourage dense wood.
NB: Do not add nitrogen fertilizers after the second month of summer, otherwise the shoots will not mature properly.

Rosa acicularis produces pear-shaped rosehips.

Rosa pimpinella altaica.

Rosa x paulii.

Hips on Rosa rugosa.

Rosa sericea pteracantha.

Hips covered in frost.

Old-fashioned charm

Species roses never fail to enchant with their simple, delicate flowers. Usually, they only flower once, in the spring, but do so in great profusion. In the autumn, they delight us with their crop of beautiful rosehips in glowing colours from red to orange. Nearly all species of roses come well armed. Their shoots bear thorns in a great variety of shapes, such as the needle-shaped bristles on *Rosa x paulii* or the red-winged ones on *Rosa sericea pteracantha*.

Rose care through the year

The following monthly summary will ensure that you do all you need to make your roses flourish as you work your way through one whole year in the rose garden. There is always something to do!

1 Remove deadheads from Polyantha roses.

In early spring

Remove winter protection: Towards the end of the first month of spring, when frost is no longer forecast, remove brushwood and

2 Remove deadheads from grafted roses.

In mid to late winter

Winter protection: If you did not carry out protective measures in autumn, you will have to do this now.
After a fall of snow knock the snow off laden branches to prevent them from snapping.

distribute any heaped up soil around the plant.
Loosen the soil: Use a fork or large hoe to work the soil to a depth of about 10 cm (4 in). Remove weeds.
Fertilizing: Fertilize in frost-free weather.
Pruning: Begin pruning when the temperature begins to rise and the buds start developing.

In the second month of spring

Pruning: Carry out the main pruning.
Loosen soil: Hoe the soil again. Remove weeds.
Mulching: After pruning, begin mulching.

In the last month of spring
(illustration 3)

Loosen the soil: Loosen the soil again if you are not mulching.
Check the roses: Look for pests and disease. Cut off infested parts and destroy them. Spray if necessary. Treat varieties susceptible to fungi every fourteen days.
Remove suckers: Cut them off near to the ground (illustration 3).
Planting: Prune roses planted in the spring and water frequently.

In the first and second months of summer
(illustrations 1 and 2)

Fertilizing: Fertilize again before the first flowering. From the middle of the

second month of summer no longer give nitrogen fertilizer so that the shoots can mature before the onset of winter.
Watering: Water during extended periods of dry weather.
Cut off deadheads: Do not deadhead roses that flower only once as they should be allowed to produce rosehips in the autumn. Roses that flower several times should be deadheaded so that they can develop new flowerbuds.
● Polyantha and Floribunda roses: Cut off the flower cluster above the first leaf. The best formed buds will be found in its axil (illustration 1).
● Hybrid tea roses: Cut away dead flowers together with two

3 Remove suckers at the point of emergence.

4 Hoe regularly but shallowly to remove weeds.

complete leaves above the third leaf and slightly at an angle away from the bud (illustration 2). Here you will find fully developed buds which will soon begin to shoot.
● Continuously flowering shrub roses: Regularly remove deadheads together with two leaves. In the case of roses that produce clusters of flowers, cut off the individual dead flowers. Do not remove the entire cluster above the first bud until all the flowers in it have died.
Tying up shoots: Fasten the shoots of climbing roses to an espalier.

In the last month of summer

Plant protection: Now is the time to watch out

for black spot. Remove infested leaves and cut off very diseased shoots. Spray if necessary.
Pruning: In the case of once-flowering, small-flowered climbing roses, carry out summer pruning immediately after flowering to encourage the formation of new annual shoots.

In the first month of autumn

Remove deadheads: Cut off dead flowers after the flowering phase of once-flowering climbing roses. Young shoots will then mature better and are less susceptible to mildew.
Fertilizing: In moist, warm weather and with continued growth, nourish the soil with a

potassium/magnesium mixture. This will help the plant to store water and growth will gradually cease. The bark will become dense and the plant will be more resistant to frost. Do not work the soil any further so that no more nitrogen is released.

In the second month of autumn

Pruning: Carry out pruning on standard roses and shape them. For all other roses only remove deadheads.
Planting: Plant new roses now.
Replanting: Transplant healthy older roses to new positions.

In the last month of autumn

Mulching: Spread well-rotted manure or garden compost if you have not mulched in the spring.
Winter protection: Depending on the climate and region, heap up soil around the roses. Collect fallen leaves and destroy them to avoid the spread of disease.
Pruning: Very long

shoots can be shortened a little before winter. Cut back a third of the crowns of standards if you have not already done this. Cut off frozen flowers and fruits.

In the first month of winter
(illustration 5)

Winter protection: Carry out winter protection measures before the middle of the first month of winter.
● Heap up soil and protect plants with brushwood or sacking.
● Wrap brushwood around the stems of young standard roses and heap soil around the lower parts.
● Older roses may also be overwintered in a wire cage filled with dead leaves (illustration 5).

5 Overwintering in a cage of dead leaves.

Creating the right shape

You will have no problem in creating standards with round, dense crowns or low-growing rose borders if you use your secateurs the right way. Using the relevant pruning methods, you can encourage your roses to grow well and flower abundantly. The following pages will prove to you that the art of pruning is not as complicated as you might think.

Above: Climbing rose "Bantry Bay" in full bloom.
Left: Climbing roses (from left to right) "Morning Jewel", and "François Juronville" with the shrub rose "Carola" at the front.

Pruning measures

Why pruning is necessary

Garden roses still need pruning even though they manage to grow quite well in the wild without our help.

The shape: Species roses do not require pruning as a rule, apart from the removal of old and diseased shoots. The idea is to allow them to develop their natural shape. Things are a little different with the other groups of roses which are planted for different reasons: a standard is intended to provide an attractive eye-catching feature; shrub roses are meant to blend into an attractive group together with other plants. In order to achieve these goals, you need to keep a check on your roses and use your secateurs.

Willingness to flower: The number of flowers will depend on the number of buds that grow in the axil of each shoot and leaf stalk. Many buds promise abundant flowers. The higher the leaf buds are situated, the faster they will develop. The dormant buds tend to be sited nearer the ground, at first appearing as merely little red dots. If you cut away the fat buds, it will take some time before the dormant buds develop and finally start shooting. The onset of flowering will be later. If you cut off the rose plant just above the soil, it has to shoot out of "blind" buds that are not yet visible. This process will take a long time as

the blind buds have to develop first into dormant buds and finally into shooting buds. The result of all this is delayed growth with a late flowering.

My tip: Cuts made above the fat buds lead to faster growth and earlier flowering.

The main pruning

Depending on the climate and altitude, the main pruning for roses should be undertaken between the first and second months of spring. Wait for the moment when the buds are beginning to swell in the lower parts of the plant. This will give you a clearer picture of the condition of the wood and the actual shooting buds and determine where you should cut (see pp. 34 and 35).

The summer cut

During the summer proper pruning will not be necessary. The exceptions to this rule are the once-flowering, small-flowered climbing roses. These should be pruned from the last month of summer until the beginning of the first month of autumn, immediately after flowering, in order to encourage the formation of new annual shoots. In the case of roses that flower more often, regular removal of dead flowers will

encourage further flowers to develop.

The autumn cut

If you decide to do the main pruning in the autumn, the rose will continue to grow on frost-free days. When there is another frost, however, freshly pruned shoots may freeze right back to the dormant buds. In the autumn, therefore, roses should not be pruned right back, only shortened a little.

● Frozen flowers and fruit should be cut off.
● The shoots of young standard roses should be cut back by a third of their length. Winter protection measures will prevent death through freezing (see overwintering, p. 42).

My tip: Always use perfectly functioning, clean, well-sharpened tools so that the roses are not damaged unnecessarily. Disease-promoting organisms will find it easier to penetrate dirty or damaged surfaces.

Getting rid of pruning refuse

When you have finished pruning, carefully gather up all the bits and dispose of them in your dustbin or burn them. Under no circumstances should they be put on your compost heap. Nor should you allow them to drop down and remain in the bed. This could cause fungal diseases to spread, which, in extreme cases, may lead to the death of the rose or of a whole rose bed.

Pruning

Pruning should be undertaken particularly carefully for bedding roses which flower on one-year-old wood, in contrast to the once-flowering bush and climbing roses which flower on old wood (see p. 34). Pruning encourages new shoots and branches to form and, with them, many more leaves. The leaves absorb carbon dioxide (CO_2) from the air and, with the help of light, chlorophyll and water, convert it to carbohydrates (sugar). At the same time oxygen is released back into the atmosphere. The total process is referred to as photosynthesis. An abundance of healthy leaves guarantees vigorous growth and a wealth of flowers.
Severe pruning: Generally speaking, many careful prunings are preferable to one radical one.

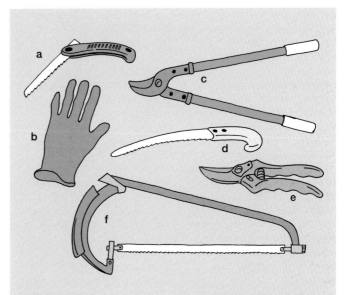

The right tools

Roses produce wood that is sensitive to pressure. Injuries scar over slowly or not at all. This means that well-maintained tools are extremely important.
Secateurs (e) are the main tool. They are suitable for cutting young as well as old shoots and for more delicate operations like cutting off deadheads.
A tree saw (d) is needed for removing tough old shoots and withered wood.
A folding saw (a) with an adjustable handle makes it possible to remove thin shoots from inaccessible places

without damaging the wood.
A branch cutter (c) is suitable for cutting stronger shoots. Rose branches with a diameter of up to 5 cm (2 in) can be cut through cleanly by exerting pressure on the extended handles.
A tree saw (f) with a bow handle ensures that you can make an exact cut even in the centre of the rose bush. Its handle can be adjusted to an angle of 90 degrees.

NB: Wear gloves (b) to protect your hands from injury. Store all tools in a safe place (see Author's notes on p. 61).

The right shape

● Vigorous cutting back will be required if you want to use hybrid tea roses as cut flowers. Thorough pruning will encourage the development of tall, barely branching stems with attractive solitary flowers.

● Freshly planted roses should also be pruned back well. If you do not do this they will not have enough energy to absorb nutrients for growth and flowers as the necessary fine roots have not yet developed.

My tip: When planting in spring, you should cut back the roses beforehand. If they are planted in the autumn they should not be cut back until the following spring.

Further pruning measures

Development cut: This will help the young rose to develop an ideal shape of growth. Only five of the best-developed shoots should remain. All others, including shoots that are too close together, should be cut away.

Shaping cut: If you consider the layout of the garden, the size of the garden and the types of plants that the roses will be growing next to, you will be able to decide how each rose should be shaped; for example, whether it should be cut into a spherical shape.

Thinning out cut: Bedding, climbing, shrub and standard roses should be thinned out every year around the end of the first month of spring; bush roses more, bedding roses less.

● All frozen, weak and sick shoots should be cut back to healthy wood (see p. 34).

● Branches that grow diagonally or towards the centre, which would interfere with an open shape and also hinder the free circulation of air and penetration of light should be cut out.

Rejuvenating cut: This should be applied to all roses if the plants are becoming too dense, which means that younger branches are being deprived of nutrients, or if plants are visibly growing less or have become bare at the bottom. As a general rule, do this every two to three years. This type of cut encourages the formation of new shoots and the life of the rose is extended.

● One-year-old shoots growing from the base should be left.

● Older, very woody shoots that no longer bear many flowers should be cut back to 20-30 cm (8-12 in).

Cut flowers

Varieties with large gaps between their leaves are very suitable for cut flowers. Cut the flowers off with as short a stem as possible, taking only about six leaves. Never cut more than three roses from one plant to avoid creating ugly stumps.

● Remove leaves and thorns from the part of the stem that will sit under water. Do not damage the bark.

● Cut the end of the stem with a knife in such a way that a long, slanting surface is obtained. This will make the cut flower last longer.

Removing suckers

Nearly all roses are created by grafting on to species stocks (see p. 7). If they are planted properly, the grafting point will be about 5 cm (2 in) beneath the surface of the soil. Very often, suckers grow below this point. They will absorb nutrients from the root. If suckers are not removed, a large, wild rose bush will grow up which, in time, will overgrow the grafted rose and kill it. In the case of standard roses, suckers may form directly below the grafting point. If they are not removed, they will slowly grow right up over the crown.

Recognizing suckers: Compared to normal rose shoots, suckers have an uneven number of smaller leaves (usually seven), are light green in colour and have more thorns.

The right way to remove suckers
Suckers are removed in the last month of spring. First clear away soil etc. around the point where

The profusely flowering "Veilchenblau" will climb vigorously over bowers, pergolas and even trees.

the sucker emerges. Then separate the sucker from the stem at the point where it emerges, using sharp secateurs or a sharp knife. This will prevent suckers from regrowing.

NB: Never cut off suckers above the soil. This would encourage them to produce new, even stronger shoots.

Prevention: Before planting, thoroughly check the roots for signs of developing suckers. Cut them away, together with a little bark, where they emerge, using a knife or secateurs. New suckers will then not form.

"Madame Isaak Pereire"

Pruning

The following information and step-by-step illustrations will demonstrate the correct way to prune roses.

Important terms

Knot: Circular swellings of the bark at the point where a lateral shoot grows from a stem.
Buds: The buds of shoots that are situated in leaf axils.
Wood: One-year-old shoots are referred to as "new" wood; wood that is several years old is "old" wood.
Pith: Storage tissue inside the twigs. It is protected by the bark.

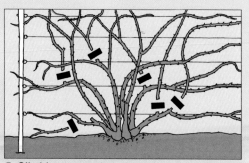

5 Climbing roses: *tie up long shoots; cut shorter shoots to two to four buds. Cut out cross shoots.*

Stump: A short length of shoot that has no buds. Stumps tend to die off which means that the part of a shoot below one may become damaged.

Pruning techniques
(illustrations 1–4)

The cut should be made barely 1 cm (less than ½ in) above a bud. The last bud should point outwards in order to maintain a direction of growth facing outwards. Shoots growing inwards interfere with an open structure.
My tip: Make the cut slanting slightly away from the bud so that rainwater can run off and not cause decay.

● Shoots that are close together and form an axil (forked branches) should be removed (illustration 2). Only a shoot pointing outward should remain. Branches that grow close together will not develop properly.
● Remove short lateral stumps close to a fork (illustration 3) as they are at risk from frost and decay.
● Sick and weak shoots should be removed. The swellings where the shoot emerged should remain (illustration 4). New shoots will grow out of these.
● Frost-damaged shoots (brownish-coloured pith) should be cut back to healthy wood (white to light green pith).

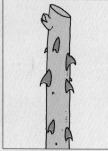

1 Correct pruning:
1 cm above a bud.

2 Forks: *remove shoots that are close together.*

3 Stump: *remove a short piece of shoot.*

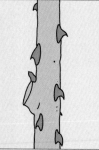

4 *Allow a small piece to remain.*

Species roses

Most species do not need pruning. In the spring, only cut back frost-damaged shoots to the healthy wood. Regularly prune species that have developed out of shrub rose varieties (see right).

Climbing roses
(illustration 5)

The long main shoots that are intended to climb along railings, pergolas and arches should not be cut back. *Often-flowering climbing roses* will also flower from new wood. Remove clusters of flowers after they have faded. Cut lateral shoots back to two to four buds. Use long laterals as new main shoots. If necessary, carry out a thinning or rejuvenating cut (see p. 32). *Once-flowering climbing roses* flower on old wood and should only be thinned out or rejuvenated. Prune immediately after flowering. The young shoots are then able to mature more easily before the autumn.

6 Bedding roses: shorten to three to eight buds.

NB: Do not cut off deadheads of varieties that produce hips.

Bedding roses
(illustration 6)

● Slow-growing varieties should be cut back to three to four buds (10-15 cm/4-6 in) They will then form stronger branches.
● Medium-fast-growing varieties should be cut back to four to six buds (15-25 cm/6-10 in).
● Fast-growing varieties should be cut back to about eight buds per shoot. If they require a rejuvenating cut, prune them the same way as slow-growing bedding roses.

Shrub roses
(illustration 7)

● Shoots that often produce flowers should not be pruned so much; weaker shoots should be cut back more (to about three to four buds). Carry out a rejuvenating cut about every three to five years, removing shoots that grow across. Old branches should be cut close to the ground.
● Once-flowering shoots should not be cut back otherwise they will not produce abundant flowers. Only thin out and, if necessary, rejuvenate.

7 Shrub roses: shorten old branches.

Standards and cascades
(illustration 8)

Standard roses: Keep the crown compact. Varieties with soft shoots should only be thinned out, all others should be cut back lightly before overwintering. Shorten shoots to 15-20 cm (6-8 in) in mid spring.
My tip: Cut main shoots above a bud growing outwards. This ensures that the centre of the crown will continue to receive enough light and young laterals will grow more easily.
Cascade roses: Only thin out.

8 Standards: shorten to 15-20 cm (6-8 in).

Roses in winter

If you have provided the ideal position for the roses in your garden and encouraged them to flower abundantly by caring for them correctly, you will also wish to do everything in your power to overwinter them in the best possible circumstances in order to watch them bloom again the following year. How to do this is described in the following pages.

Above: A late autumn rose covered in frost.
Left: The scented shrub rose "Schneewittchen" in the form of tall standards, framed by lady's mantle (Alchemilla mollis).

Safely through the winter

When to give winter protection

Most indigenous species roses will not require any winter protection because, as a rule, they are completely hardy. It is different, however, for rose species which do not originate in Europe, as well as for many bedding, shrub, climbing and standard roses. They will all require wrapping up during the winter (see pp. 42 and 43).

When to begin: You should start to prepare your roses for the winter from the middle of the last month of autumn to the beginning of the first month of winter. If you start any earlier, parts of the rose wood will not have matured properly and the wood will be too soft. A light frost now and again will not damage roses in this transitional period. Only when continuous frost is forecast will you need to take precautions for winter protection.

Natural protection: Dry snow that contains plenty of air will not conduct heat very well and therefore will not allow the remaining warmth in the soil to escape too easily. For this reason, it will provide some protection for roses. Unfortunately, nature does not always ensure that there will be sufficient snow in all regions at risk from frost, so you should definitely take additional measures to provide protection against the cold.

Protection from winter sun

Frost will actually damage your roses far less than the extreme temperature swings that can occur in late winter and spring.

● When sunny days follow cold, frosty nights, the dormant shoots of the roses are persuaded to begin to shoot. During the daytime, the warm rays of the sun encourage sap to flow through the shoots, but then, at night, it is frozen. The cell walls expand, the bark bursts and the branches die off. When the sun is very intense, just a few hours will be enough to create terrific tension in the tissues of branches.

● Strong sunlight and cold northerly and easterly winds encourage the evaporation of water stored in the rose's branches. If the soil is frozen at the same time, the rose can no longer replenish its water supply through its roots. There is an acute lack of moisture that will cause the plant to dry up.

Preparatory measures

The following measures should be undertaken prior to overwintering.

● Cease fertilizing the soil with nitrogen in the middle of the second month of summer at the latest so that the shoots of the rose may mature properly before the onset of winter and so that the plant will cease growing at the correct time (see p. 24).

● Do not work the soil any more from the first month of autumn onwards so that no more nitrogen is released.

● During the end of autumn and beginning of winter, collect all fallen leaves and dispose of them in a refuse sack or, if possible, burn them. They are not suitable for composting as they are often infested with black spot spores that would overwinter in the compost and promote the next attack of the disease.

● The roses should not be pruned until the spring (see p. 30). Before the winter, only shorten very long shoots a little and cut back the crowns of standards by about a third. Remove all deadheads and dead leaves from your roses and dispose of them.

Heaping up soil

Overwintering roses can begin with the heaping up of soil. This includes creating a ring of garden soil (which may be enriched with ripe compost) around the neck of the roots to a height of 20-30 cm (8-12 in), a bit like a mole hill. The ground beneath the grafting point will thus be protected so that it cannot freeze.

NB: Do not use the soil that is already around the rose plant for heaping up. Hoeing it up could easily accidentally expose the roots and damage them. It is better to obtain the soil from another part of the garden. Also do not use peat as it would soak up water and have the effect of an ice-pack on your roses during frosty weather.

My tip: In the case of bedding plants, the furrows between the rows of roses should be covered up with a mixture of old, straw-rich stable manure, rotted leaves or bark mulch. This will provide additional protection for the roses and encourage soil organisms.

Material for covering roses

Another trick of successful overwintering is laying down conifer branches or using sacking.

Firwood is particularly good as the needles will drop by the spring. Air and sunlight will then be able to penetrate to the shoots and benefit your roses.

Sacking is excellent for wrapping around standards.

Overwintering rose arches

Climbing roses in open positions are particularly at risk from frost. The changes between sunshine, drying wind and low temperatures at night will all affect the rose plants. In addition, the plant will lose lots of moisture through evaporation and the roots will be unable to replenish it from the frozen ground. Without protection, the shoots will dry up and die back right down to the ground. Rose arches require a roof-like covering in winter to protect them from both sunshine and wind. Melted snow and rainwater will also be able to run off well.

Materials: For covering use a thick bundle of pine or fir branches (depending on the size of the arch), along with string for tying the branches together and tying them around the arch.

Procedure: The best way to carry out the job is for one person to lean on the branches and hold them in position while another person wraps the string around and ties it up.

● Shoots that spread too far apart should be tied together with string beforehand.

● Start tying on branches at the base of the rose arch and work your way upwards. The

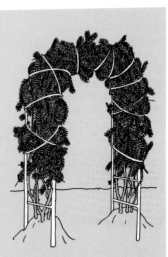

stems of the branches should point upwards.

● The second row should be tied on slightly higher, so that the branches overlap like fish scales.

● You can then wrap string loosely around this layer and thereby secure the lower branches even more.

● Carry on adding rows of branches right to the top centre of the arch. Carry on wrapping the string around so that the branches are loosely tied over the rose shoots.

● Wrap up the other side of the rose arch in the same manner.

● Close the gap in the middle with brushwood and tie it up.

● Heap up a little soil at the foot of each base to protect the roots.

Safely through the winter

You may also use baling fabric. This loose-mesh jute fabric is used for wrapping up rootstocks in tree nurseries.

NB: Polythene is not suitable for winter protection. In milder winter weather, heat will be stored underneath it and this will encourage the rose to shoot early and weaken its natural resistance. Night frosts would then be able to inflict a lot of harm.

During the winter

Snowfalls: After heavy snowfalls in the winter, remove the weight of snow from the roses to prevent branches from snapping off. This danger is greater if the snow is wet and heavy.

Roof avalanches: Remember that roses planted close to the house are at risk from avalanches of snow. As soon as the snow begins to thaw, great masses of snow may slide from your roof. Protect your roses by building tent-like structures with planks and posts before the winter begins.

Salt damage: If you have a fence with climbing roses or a rose hedge beside a busy road, the plants may well suffer during the winter whenever salt is strewn. Protective cane matting can be installed along the side nearer the road to prevent sprays of wet slush mixed with salt from showering your roses.

Removing winter protection

Towards the end of the first month of spring, roughly about the same time as forsythia is flowering, you can remove the winter protection from your roses. If you wait any longer, the shoots will grow too fast under their cover and remain too soft. This, in turn, would heighten susceptibility to diseases. Choose a day that is dull for this job so that the roses are not immediately confronted with bright sunlight.

● Any planks that were positioned to protect the roses from roof avalanches can now be removed.

● Coverings of conifer brushwood as well as sacking should be carefully removed so that the shooting buds are not damaged.

● Once no more frosty nights are forecast, heaped up soil around the plant can be carefully removed with a hoe and distributed. The mulching layer in the furrows of rose beds can be evened out and covered with garden soil. This will encourage rapid rotting. The layer will be transformed into humus and will also work like fertilizer. Additional loosening of the soil with a large hoe or garden fork will improve the oxygen supply to the root system of the rose plants.

● Young standards should be left lying flat for a few days in their prostrate winter position after the winter protection covering has been removed, before they are very carefully lifted up again and tied to a post.

● Roses in large containers can now be dug up again and placed in a bright, but not too sunny position. If there are any more unexpected night frosts, take the plants inside for the night.

● The cane matting protecting a rose hedge and fence can also be removed now.

Redesigning your garden

If you have taken photos of your garden regularly during the spring and summer, you can spend some time in the winter on planning the basic redesigning and restructuring of beds. Study the colours and shapes of your roses and companion plants throughout the year. If you wish to make changes – either simple or more radical – now is the time to make your plans.

Many adult education and gardening societies offer courses and talks for amateur gardeners during the winter and you may find some that include the care of roses.

In early summer shrub rose "Fritz Nobis" produces its abundant flowers and wonderful scent.

Overwintering

Your roses will survive the winter safely if they are properly protected. Cold weather, snow, ice and also wind and sunshine in late winter and very early spring will not be able to harm the roses if you stick to a few basic rules.

Bedding and shrub roses
(illustration 2)

Hardy bedding and shrub roses do not require any winter covering. If, however, some of the shoots are damaged by frost, they should be cut back to healthy wood in the spring (see p. 30). They

will eventually start shooting vigorously again.

Non-hardy varieties should be protected as follows:

● Heap up soil around the base of the rose to a height of 20-30 cm (8-12 in) (see p. 38). This will protect the neck of the root and the grafting point which should be located about 5 cm (2 in) beneath the surface of the soil if the rose has been planted correctly.

● Cover the rose with a loose layer of conifer branches to protect it from intense winter sunlight and cold easterly winds. You may also push branches into

the soil heap around the rose and in between the shoots. Alternatively, use sacking or straw as covering.

Climbing roses
(illustration 3)

Among the climbers, varieties that are not hardy will also require some winter protection.

● Heap soil more generously around climbing roses than around bedding roses – about 40 cm (16 in) – as they are subject to great fluctuations in temperature when planted on an espalier directly against a wall.

● In addition to the soil heap, distribute a protective layer of compost all around the neck of the root (to a diameter of 70 cm /28in).

● Climbing shoots can be protected by arranging conifer branches up to a height of about 1 m (40 in) in overlapping layers. Either tie the branches to the espalier or draw them through the mesh of the fence.

Rose arches should be covered from top to

bottom with brushwood and have soil heaped up around the base.

Standards
(illustrations 1 and 5)

Standards will need special winter

2 Bedding roses are protected with heaped soil and brushwood.

protection as their grafting point is situated directly beneath the crown at the top end of the stem and this will react very sensitively to cold or drying winds.

Young standards (see illustration 1)

● Remove any remaining leaves and shoot tips before overwintering so that no decay can occur in the covered-up crown of the tree. Cut back the

1 Young standards can be bent over and anchored with wire. Heap soil over the crown and the roots.

shoots slightly (see p. 30).
● Cover the stem with dense brushwood or sacking.
NB: Make sure that the sensitive grafting point right at the base of the crown is well covered with soil.

3 Climbing roses can be covered over a large surface area.

● On the side where the young tree is going to be bent downwards loosen the root area a little with a garden fork, then, very gently, press the pliable young stem down to the soil.
● Clamp the standard's stem to the ground using a forked branch, bent coathanger or crossed sticks.
● Cover the crown completely, to above

the grafting point, with loose soil.
● Heap soil up around the foot.
My tip: Do not dig out a depression for the crown. This would cause water to collect which would soon encourage the shoots to rot.
Older standards
(see illustration 5)
● The stem of an older standard will no longer bend so it must be completely covered with conifer brushwood or sacking. Heap plenty of soil around the foot.
● Wrap up the slightly cut back crown area and the grafting point in conifer branches. Finally, draw a jute sack over the protective wrapping and tie up well with string.
My tip: Older standards can also be protected by building a cage of wire around them and filling this with straw or dead leaves until the crown is no longer visible (see p. 27). Before you add the filling, tie the shoots loosely together.

4 Container roses can be sunk into the ground.

Species roses

Species roses that originate from the European continent are, as a rule, hardy and will not require any winter protection.
In severe winters, some shoots may freeze but these can be cut back to healthy wood in the spring. Non-European species roses that are sensitive to frost, as well as grafted species roses, such as bedding and shrub roses, will need protection.

Roses in large containers
(illustration 4)

Large container roses, which you would prefer to overwinter in the

garden rather than in the house, should not be left outside without any winter protection. The relatively small amount of soil in a free-standing pot will not prevent the rootstock from freezing up.
Planting in a soil bed
● First cut back the plant by about a third.
● Dig out a spacious pit to a depth of about 60-80 cm (24-32 in) to accommodate the pot.
● Carefully line the walls of the pit with thick cardboard or wooden panels.
● Stand the rose in its container in the pit, heap soil into and around it and cover everything with a 20 cm (8 in) thick layer of straw or fine brushwood as well as conifer branches.

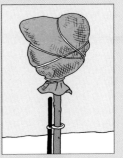

5 Older standards are protected with sacking.

Healthy roses

Every rose lover is looking for completely
healthy roses all around the garden. In
spite of the careful choice of varieties
and position, the plants will never be
quite safe from diseases and pests. The
following pages will tell you how to use
preventive measures and what to do in an
emergency.

Above: The shrub rose "Erfurt".
*Left: Attractive companion planting: bedding rose
"Gruss an Bayern" in brilliant red framed by
lavender and larkspur.*

45

Healthy roses

Prevention is better than cure

Plant protection begins right from the day you purchase your roses. Choose a robust variety, preferably one recommended by a reputable grower (see p. 16).

Position: Roses require an airy, sunny position where heat is not stored or trapped. Do not plant them in waterlogged soils or, if you do, provide drainage beforehand.

Preparing the soil: A loose, air-permeable soil with good drainage properties is important, as is covering the soil with mulching material. These measures will help to combat pests (see pp. 20/21).

Fertilizing: Balanced fertilizing is also important for the maintenance of healthy roses (see p. 24). This can be carried out according to the requirements of the plant after a soil analysis has been undertaken. Too many, or not enough, nutrients will make roses susceptible to disease (see p. 55).

Pruning: Correct pruning will also provide protection against diseases (see pp. 30-35). Weak, dried-up and frost-damaged branches should be removed so that nutrients can penetrate the healthy parts of the plant and work to strengthen it.

Companion planting: The neighbouring plants growing under and around a group of roses may help to keep away pests and fungi (see p. 55).

Natural plant fortifiers: If your roses become sick in spite of all these preventive measures, do not immediately resort to chemical plant protection agents. For as long as possible try to use environmentally friendly plant fortification agents (brews and fermented brews, see p. 50). The useful insects that occur naturally in the garden (see pp. 52/53) can also often work wonders.

Plant protection agents: If all else fails, you may need to resort to biological plant protection preparations bought in the gardening trade, and in extreme cases even to chemical agents (see p. 51). You can use fungicides against fungal diseases; biting and sucking insects can be combated with insecticides; mites with acaricides. Only ever use bee-friendly preparations that work selectively; that is, that are targeted against one disease or pest. Get advice from a good garden centre.

Diseases

The more carefully you check your roses the sooner you will recognise pests and diseases and the sooner you will be able to do something effective.

Fungal diseases: These are parasitic diseases that mostly occur in conditions of high humidity and warmth. They often infest soft plant tissue that has been given too much nitrogen fertilizer. The fungi grow into the cell tissue of the plants and extract nutrients from them. Propagation occurs in the form of spores transported by moving air. This results in a rapid spread of the problem.

● Black spot, rust and powdery mildew often occur in roses (see p. 48).

● Rust: The main characteristic of this problem lies in the fact that the fungal spores use another plant species, for example, juniper, as an in-between host, therefore never plant juniper near roses.

● Downy mildew: This will spread rapidly in wet summers. First a greyish-white covering of mould develops on the undersides of leaves and, later, brownish to reddish spots occur. Partial loss of foliage is one result. Plant in an airy position, collect any fallen leaves and destroy them.

● Sooty mould: This fungus likes to colonize the honeydew excretions of aphids and scale insects and forms a sticky blackish film on the leaves. Combat the insects by spraying the roses with a soap and spirit solution.

● Grey mould: Botrytis fungus infests the buds, flowers, leaves and shoots. They begin to decay. After a while, a film of light grey mould appears. In addition, brown decaying patches often appear that lead to the rapid wilting and dying of parts of the plant. Ensure plenty of ventilation and use balanced fertilizers. Spray plants with mare's tail brew. Cut off infected parts and destroy them.

Viral diseases: Usually, the virus is transmitted by sucking insects like aphids and leafhoppers or by using infected cutting tools. The result is lack of flower formation, sparse growth and damage to chlorophyll (shown by light and dark areas on leaves). Always disinfect tools carefully. Combat insects that transmit the disease and destroy affected plants.

The correct position

If you make sure that light and air can penetrate your roses and that they are not smothered by neighbouring plants and are properly pruned, you will do a lot to prevent the worst effects of disease.

Animal pests

These may proliferate rapidly. *Insects:* These will damage cultivated plants through their biting and sucking activities. As caterpillars and larvae they will eat foliage, young shoots, roots or buds. They will transmit viral disease during this time.

● The most commonly occurring harmful insects include aphids, scale insects, leaf wasps, thrips and sawflies (see pp. 49 and 52).

● Tortrix moth: This small moth deposits its eggs singly on branches where they are left to overwinter. In the spring, brownish caterpillars hatch that may grow up to 15 mm (1 in) long. They will eat the leaves and petals, spin a web around individual leaves and form chrysalises inside. Remove webs and rolled leaves and destroy them. Treat with insecticide if the infestation is severe.

● Winter moth caterpillars: These green caterpillars propel themselves along by arching their bodies. They will eat leaves, buds and young shoots. Cut off infested leaves and shoots and destroy them.

● Bedeguar gall wasp: This insect lays its eggs mainly in the shoots of species roses; the shoot then swells and develops a greenish-red, ball-shaped structure (Robin's pincushion). Whitish larvae grow inside the gall. The part of the shoot above the gall usually dies off. Cut off and destroy galls.

Spider mites: These are not true insects. They belong to the group of arachnids to which spiders also belong and they are extremely small. The worst pest is the red spider mite (see p. 52) which sucks the sap from plants so that parts become yellow and drop off. It is extremely active on hot, dry, summer days.

Pests in the roots: Nematodes (eelworms) are recognisable by their snake-like movements. These 0.5-2 mm long, colourless, almost transparent creatures live a parasitic life in the root tissue. They cause stunted growth and swellings among the roots. Infested plants or stocks should be removed. You should then plant species like marigold in this site for several years to get rid of the nematodes.

Common pests and diseases

Planting in the right position will decrease the susceptibility of roses to pests and diseases. However, even the more robust varieties growing on good soil may still have problems. Unfavourable weather conditions, for example, moist, warm weather or a long drought, will challenge roses. Infestation with disease or pests generally begins with just a few conspicuous symptoms. It is therefore very important to check your roses regularly. Only in this way will you be able to control the problem in time.

Black spot

Symptoms: Irregular, blackish patches on the leaves. The leaves turn yellow and drop off. This great loss of leaves weakens the rose, so new wood is unable to mature and become hardy.

Cause: A fungal infection on leaves and roots through insufficient fertilizing, damp weather and wet soil.

Remedy: Plant resistant varieties; use balanced fertilizing; remove and destroy affected leaves; spray with mare's tail brew; spray with agents containing sulphur at intervals of ten days.

Rose rust

Symptoms: Rusty yellow patches on the uppersides of leaves; the undersides have orange-red, powdery pustules, which turn black in the autumn; falling leaves.

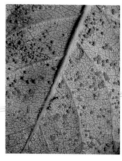

Cause: A fungal infection in warm, dry weather.

Remedy: Prevent by spraying with wormwood and mare's tail brew; cut out and destroy infested leaves.

Powdery mildew

Symptoms: Whitish-grey, floury film on the top and undersides of leaves, shoots and buds. The leaves become crippled, but do not generally drop off. The wood does not mature. Sparse growth of affected shoots and flowers.

Cause: Fungal infection through excessively high doses of nitrogen; muggy weather with high humidity and very little movement of air.

Remedy: Plant in airy positions; spray with mare's tail brew or fermented nettle brew; in the autumn, cut off infested shoots right back to healthy wood and destroy them; spray with anti-mildew agents at intervals of ten days during an infestation.

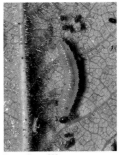

Thrips

Symptoms: Silvery, usually dark-edged patches on leaves and petals. The buds open with difficulty and may become crippled.
Cause: Damage caused by sucking. There may

be a massive proliferation of thrips during warm, dry conditions.
Remedy: Cut off and destroy infested buds.

Rose sawfly

Symptoms: Wilting of individual shoot tips. The leaves on these dry up. The shoots die off.
Cause: In the spring, the sawflies lay their eggs on the shoot tips or at the base of leaf stalks. The larvae bore a hole and enter the pith. They turn a whitish yellow colour and eat their way down or up the shoot (see photograph above).
Remedy: Cut back infested shoots to healthy wood and burn the refuse before the larvae are able to escape from it. Hang up nesting boxes for birds.

Rose leafhopper

Symptoms: White spots and fine white patches on the uppersides of leaves. The leaves dry up and fall off. Leafhoppers often occur in dry, warm positions.

Cause: Whitish to light green insects suck the sap from cells along the veins on the undersides of leaves.
Remedy: Spray undersides of leaves with insecticide.

Leaf-rolling rose sawfly

Symptoms: Individual leaves roll up to the central vein like a tube and become unable to function. They turn yellow and die off prematurely.
Cause: During the last month of spring the leaf-rolling rose sawfly lays its eggs along the edges of the leaves which then roll inwards. Inside, the whitish to light-green larva can develop undisturbed. It attains a length of about 9 mm by the end of the first month of summer.
Remedy: In the case of sporadic appearances, cut off the infested leaves and destroy them. If infestation is severe, spray with agents containing pyrethrum (see p. 54). Make sure the undersides of the leaves are well soaked.

Healthy roses

Fortifying plants the natural way

Diseases and pests on roses can definitely be tackled with biological methods. Relevant preparations can be obtained in the gardening trade (see p. 51) but you can also prepare your own washes and fermented brews and employ them preventively as well as to combat infestation. The following are a few useful recipes.

Mare's tail brew

This concoction will help to fortify the plant tissue and also combat mildew, rust and red spider mite.
Preparation: Take a wooden or plastic container, fill it with 1 kg (2 lb) fresh or 150 g (5 oz) dried mare's tail and add 10 litres (18 pt) cold water. Allow it to soak for about 24 hours then cover and simmer on a medium heat for 30 minutes so that the silicic acid can separate out as an active ingredient. Cover again and allow to cool. Strain the liquid into a second wooden or plastic container. Use one part of brew diluted with five parts' water for spraying.
Use: As a preventive measure, spray the entire plant before the heat of midday on extremely hot days (for maximum effect of the brew). Then water the root area with the brew. If the plant is already infested, repeat the procedure several days in succession.
NB: The brew will only keep for about two weeks. When it begins to ferment, use it only as a watering additive (1 litre/2 pt brew diluted with 10 litres/18 pt water).
My tip: Do not store the brew in metal containers as the acid will corrode the metal.

Fermented nettle brew

This concoction makes a good fertilizer and will also enhance the plant's resistance to disease. It will help plants to develop a thicker epidermis as a protection against sucking insects.
Preparation: Put 500-700 g (1-1 lb 10 oz) fresh or 200 g (7 oz) dried nettles in a wooden container with 5 litres (8¾ pt) cold water. Allow it to stand for about fourteen days. Stir daily until fermentation begins (the brew no longer produces foam). Strain and pour it into storage containers. Use one part of fermented nettle brew diluted with ten parts' water.
Alternative: Use cold nettle water mixture in the same ratio. Mix as above but this time allow the mixture to stand for only 12 to 24 hours (three days at most) so that it does not begin to ferment. Use immediately.
Use: Pour on to the root area and use to spray leaves. Spray cold nettle water undiluted on to your roses to combat aphids.
NB: Ready-to-use nettle powder can be obtained in the gardening trade and should be diluted with water according to the instructions on the packet.
My tip: Mix mare's tail brew and fermented nettle brew together for an enhanced effect.

Soft soap solution

This is used against scale insects.
Preparation: Use pure soft soap purchased from a chemist. Depending on the degree of infestation, dissolve 150-300 g (5-10 oz) soap in a bucket with 10 litres (18 pt) hot water. Allow to cool.
Use: Spray undiluted all over the plant.

Spirit and soap solution

For combating aphids and scale insects.
Preparation: Dissolve 200 g (7 oz) soft soap in hot water. Dilute with 10 litres (18 pt) hot water. Add 300 ml (½ pt) methylated spirit and stir well.
Use: Spray the solution over the plant.

Biological agents for use against fungal diseases

If you do not wish to make this preparation yourself you can obtain the relevant plant protection agents in the gardening trade. Make sure, however, that you consider the welfare of the environment when using it.

Harmless: The silicic acid in mare's tail brew concentrates stabilizes the rose and helps to make it resistant to fungal diseases. Lecithin preparations, whose active ingredients are derived from soya, can be selectively employed against powdery mildew.

Slightly harmful to the environment: Sulphur-containing preparations consist of ground-up herbs like nettles, mare's tail, onions, garlic and kelp as well as 24 per cent sulphur. These will work against downy mildew and black spot. Sprays containing sulphur will, however, also damage useful predatory mites which are the natural enemies of spider mites.

NB: Agents containing copper, which are also used against fungal diseases, are toxic to the environment so do not use them. Try not to use preparations which will harm bees, fish (if you have a garden pond) or birds. Make sure none of your preparations can "stray" on to a neighbour's property etc.

A wooden tub is ideal for starting off the brew.

Wormwood brew or fermented brew

This will help to combat aphids, caterpillars and rust.
Preparation: Place 300-500 g (10½-1 lb 2 oz) fresh wormwood leaves or 30 g (about 1 oz) dried wormwood leaves in a wooden container together with 10 litres (18 pt) cold water. Allow this to stand for about a fortnight until the concoction begins to ferment. Stir daily. Mix one part with ten parts' water.
Use: Water the root area; spray the leaves.
Alternative: Cold wormwood water can be made by leaving the ingredients to stand for 24 hours so that the mixture does not begin to ferment. Use undiluted to water with in the spring.

Spraying roses with chemicals

Never resort to this unless the plant has crossed the borderline and is severely at risk. For example, if infestation with aphids has reached such a degree that the plant can no longer cope with the sheer number of pests, you will have to spray. A healthy rose should be able to cope, without human intervention, with a "normal" aphid population in a garden in a natural setting which includes naturally occurring useful insects.
Observe the following points when spraying:
● Always take the greatest precautions when using plant protection agents (see Author's notes on p. 61).
● Never spray into open blooms.
● Spray the undersides of leaves thoroughly. Pests and fungi are often found there.
● Follow the manufacturer's instructions as to dosage. (The same goes for all biological preparations too.)
● Do not breathe in the spray mist. Wear a mask and gloves.
● Store all plant protection agents in their original containers, locked away safely and inaccessible to children and domestic pets.
● Never pour remains of sprays down the drain. This is sensitive waste which should be disposed of separately.

Insects

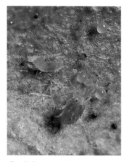

What should you do if your roses are infested with pests? To begin with, just let their natural enemies have a go. As long as useful insects and other creatures are successfully preventing them from proliferating, there is no need for you to intervene. Among the most important useful insects in your garden are ladybirds, predatory mites, lacewings and hoverflies. They will target spider mites, aphids and scale insects. For this reason, you must remember, when using chemical plant protection agents, that you may be killing useful insects as well as pests and will be leaving any survivors or newly arriving predators no food.

Aphids

Symptoms: Sucking damage on buds, shoot tips and leaf undersides; crippled parts; lack of flowers. Aphids also play a large part in spreading viral diseases.
Causes: Warm, dry weather; excessive nitrogen fertilizing.
Remedy: Ensure good ventilation; check your dose of nitrogen fertilizer; protect natural predators like ladybirds and lacewings. Initially, if there are only a few aphids, strip them off and crush them. Cut off and destroy infested leaves and shoots. Spray the plant with a soft soap solution or with fermented nettle brew. Only use chemical agents in extreme cases.

Spider mites

Symptoms: Whitish-yellow, speckled uppersides of leaves. Later, brownish discoloration. Fine webs on the undersides. The leaves dry up and drop off.

Cause: Spider mites (reddish with bristles) which suck the sap from the undersides of leaves.
Remedy: Avoid sunny, hot positions; use mare's tail brew and acaricides.

Scale insects

Symptoms: Scale insects (see photograph above) stick firmly to shoots and leaves where they suck the sap. There is honeydew formation, with a subsequent development of sooty mould. Sparse growth.
Cause: Positions that are either too dry or too humid.
Remedy: Careful selection of position; protect natural enemies like lacewings; remove scale insects mechanically with a stick or a brush; remove infested shoots and leaves; spray the plant with paraffin or tar oil. These substances will coat the scale insect and prevent it from breathing. The last resort is spraying with an insecticide.

Predatory mites

Ladybirds

Lacewings

Hoverflies

Use: Predatory mites can be employed against spider mites, particularly against red spider mite (see photograph above: a predatory mite devouring the egg of a red spider mite).
Appearance: The young are pale yellowish and turn reddish to brownish with increasing age. The body is pear-shaped and shiny smooth.
Lifestyle: Predatory mites lay their milky-white eggs in the leaf axils along the leaf veins. You can provide them with shelter made of many layers of material (for example, old nylon tights), wrapped around thick branches in several places in the garden.

Use: Ladybirds mainly live off aphids, scale insects and spider mites; the larvae are particularly voracious.
Appearance: A roundish beetle, brightly coloured with many spots.

Lifestyle: It lays its eggs on the undersides of leaves or underneath the scales of scale insects. It overwinters in such places as under heaps of dry leaves.

Use: In their larval state lacewings will attack aphids and also mites.
Appearance: Lacewings are generally greenish, with large, golden eyes and transparent wings. The yellow brown larvae, which have brownish-red stripes along their sides, possess strong sucking mouthparts.
Lifestyle: The eggs are deposited singly or in clusters on all kinds of surfaces, often in the close vicinity of aphid colonies. Overwintering takes place in frost-free nooks and crannies outside or in buildings.

Use: The larvae of hoverflies are important consumers of aphids.
Appearance: Hoverflies have a conspicuous black and yellow marked body which, unfortunately, often leads to them being confused with wasps and being killed. The larvae are greenish to yellowish.
Lifestyle: You will able to attract hoverflies to your garden with plants like parsley, caraway and coriander or with yellow-flowering *Plantago* species. They will lay their white eggs singly near colonies of aphids in the garden. Pieces of tree trunk with holes drilled into them will provide excellent winterquarters for this insect.

Healthy roses

Useful insects and other creatures

Useful helpers will appear in your garden if you abstain from using toxic chemical sprays and give the useful predators a chance to live.

Offering shelter: Install suitable accommodation for useful insects, for example, pieces of tree trunk with holes drilled into them, heaps of dead leaves or nesting boxes.

Use the right doses of fertilizer: If you fertilize plants with excessive doses of nitrogen, aphids will proliferate. Even useful insects will then no longer be able to cope with the mass of pests.

The most common useful insects include ladybirds, lacewings, hoverflies and predatory mites (see p. 53) and also the earwig (see right).

● Parasitic wasps (*Leptomastix*) lay their eggs by pushing an egg-laying spike into the egg, larva or chrysalis of other insects. The hatching larvae devour the host insect from the inside out. Parasitic wasps are very effective parasites of aphids. They overwinter under bark scales, moss and clumps of grass. Pieces of wood with holes bored in them offer excellent winter accommodation.

My tip: Check pruned plant matter before destroying it. Pick out the dark-coloured, mummified aphids in which

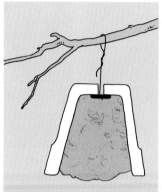

Earwigs

Earwigs have an approximately 2 cm (¾in) long, brown body with  pincers at the rear end (see left). They are useful in a rose garden as they hunt aphids, preferably at night. During the day they usually hide under fallen leaves or stones. You can provide artificial shelter by loosely filling a flowerpot with wood shavings and hanging it upside down from a branch (see above). Remove the pot in the winter and, in the spring, fill it with fresh wood shavings and hang it up again. Earwigs overwinter in the soil, providing it is left undisturbed and is not waterlogged.

parasitic wasps are overwintering and place them in a sheltered position in the garden.

● Ground beetles are nocturnal predators which devour caterpillars, aphids and mites.

● Songbirds consume insects, spiders and caterpillars. They also help with the control of winter moths. They require bushes and shrubs as a habitat. Offer nesting boxes in the spring. Not until it becomes obvious that there are not enough useful insects in your garden, should you resort to other measures. Environmentally friendly preparations to combat caterpillars can be obtained in the gardening trade. Biological plant treatment oils will help to control spider mites, scale insects and aphids.

NB: Pyrethrum preparations are often considered to be harmless and "biological". They are effective against insects and spider mites but, unfortunately, also against useful insects like parasitic wasps and ladybirds. Pyrethrum is very toxic if it reaches the nerve system via the bloodstream. Be very careful if you have any injuries or skin diseases, particularly if you also suffer from allergies. Only spray when there is no wind and always wear gloves. Read the instructions for application (see Author's notes, p. 61).

Diseases caused by mistakes in fertilizing

Roses require nutrients in particular quantities for healthy growth.

Mistakes in fertilizing can lead to nutrient lack or excess. In both cases the plant will become sick (see p. 24).

Nitrogen

● Deficiency: Weak shoots, pale green young leaves; sometimes tiny red dots are visible on the uppersides of the leaves; early loss of leaves. Use fast working liquid fertilizer or special nitrogen fertilizer.

● Excess: Too vigorous growth, soft shoots; reduced resistance; risk of mildew infestation. From the end of the first month of summer give no more nitrogen fertilizer (even earlier in the case of slow-reacting fertilizers).

Phosphorus

● Deficiency: Short, weak shoots; violet brown patches on leaf edges; reduced fruit formation. Use fast-acting, long-term-release fertilizer; phosphorus fertilizer (superphosphate).

● Excess: Metabolic disturbances. Iron and copper can no longer be absorbed. Do not use any more phosphorus fertilizer. Only use single nutrient fertilizer (N-K fertilizer).

Potassium

● Deficiency: Wilting leaves, shoots that do not mature properly; young leaves with a reddish sheen and brown edges; often on sandy soil. Use fast-acting fertilizer; potassium magnesium compound. Improve sandy soil long term with added compost.

● Excess: Cessation of growth. Stop fertilizing with potassium. Do not use multi-nutrient fertilizers.

Calcium

● Deficiency: Reduced growth of roots. Use dolomite gravel, lime, shell and kelp.

● Excess: Iron is bound in the soil. May cause chlorosis. Do not use lime as a fertilizer.

Magnesium deficiency: The leaves have "dead" zones in their centres, coloured yellowish-red; older leaves drop off first; often on acid soils. Use potassium-magnesium fertilizer; Epsom salts.

Iron deficiency (chlorosis):
Yellow leaves, only the leaf veins remain green; too much calcium is bound in the soil. Use iron fertilizer (single nutrient fertilizer).

Manganese deficiency: Yellow stripes in the spaces between leaf veins; often in older leaves. Spray with manganese sulphate.

Useful plant communities

It will, of course, be a matter of taste whether you choose to have a uniform rose bed or a planting combining roses with other shrubs and herbaceous perennials. A mixed bed is definitely healthier from the point of view of plant protection.

Lavender and gypsophila planted immediately beside roses will keep away ants and aphids.

Marigolds and tagetes around the feet of roses will keep away the toxic, water-soluble excretions of nematodes (eelworms).

Garlic is effective in controlling bacteria and fungi and as a prevention against mildew.

Nasturtium and garden cress will keep away aphids and scale insects.

Euphorbia species, for example, the roots of the decorative *Euphorbia lathyris*, offer a certain amount of protection against moles.

Both healthy and attractive in its contrasting colours is a combination of roses with ornamental sage, veronica varieties and blue green ornamental grasses. Larkspur, poppies, madonna lilies and white marguerite daisies also make good partners for roses.

Healthy roses

Ten tips on rose care

The following information covers the ten most important questions usually asked by amateur rose growers.

1 In what positions do roses thrive best?

Roses love a sunny, airy position. Rainwater should run away easily so that they do not have wet feet for lengthy periods of time. Nor do they like to be constantly bombarded by drips from neighbouring trees or to be surrounded by asphalt-covered surfaces that radiate heat and absorb moisture from the soil. On positions, see p. 20.

2 How often should roses be fertilized and how much fertilizer do they need?

Excess fertilizing will lead to excessive growth and soft shoots that are susceptible to disease. Never use the standard rule of fertilizing once or twice a year, but have your actual soil requirements established through soil analysis. Give fertilizer according to the results of this procedure.
The first dose should be given in early spring, the next one after the first flowering in early summer. Do not fertilize any more later on so that the shoots

will mature properly and become hardy. Only potassium magnesium fertilizer should be given after the second month of summer. This will encourage maturing of the wood. (See also p. 24.)

3 Is organic or mineral fertilizer more effective?

Mineral fertilizer acts faster and can be dosed more exactly, but in the long term leads to the soil being full of salts. Soil organisms will retreat or partially die off and earthworms can no longer work to produce humus. The soil's fertility is lost. Viewed long term, therefore, organic fertilizer is more advisable. The nutrients take longer to be transformed but activity in the soil increases. The soil's fertility is retained. (See also p. 24.)

4 What is wrong when roses no longer grow properly and hardly produce flowers?

After eight to ten years, roses will generally show meagre growth and reduced formation of flowers. The cause is soil exhaustion. Toxic substances are released via the rose's roots which hinder nutrient absorption. Nematodes (eelworms), unbalanced fertilizing and nutrient deficiency can also result

in sparse growth. Either exchange the soil or, better still, transfer the roses to a different bed. The wrong kind of overwintering, lack of pruning or rejuvenating cuts may cause lack of flowers. (See also pp. 23 and 31.)

5 When should roses be pruned?

The main pruning takes place in mid to late spring when night frosts can no longer inflict damage on the roses.
Young standard roses, whose crown shoots will be protected by soil during the winter, can be pruned in the autumn. A light thinning out of shrub and climbing roses is also possible in the autumn. (See also p. 30.)

6 How should roses be pruned?

This will depend on their growth. In the case of bedding roses, as a rule, fast-growing varieties are cut back less and slow-growing varieties more – depending on the degree, back to four to eight buds (about 15-20 cm/6-8 in). Thinner shoots should always be cut back further than stronger ones. Leave the long main shoots of climbing roses. The lateral shoots should be cut back to about three buds. Shrub roses should only be thinned out and rejuvenated so that they can grow naturally. (See also p. 34.)

7 Are any roses particularly easy to care for?

With the exception of species and shrub roses, roses are quite demanding. Certain rose varieties are, however, quite robust and resistant to disease. They are usually recommended by nurseries as healthy and hardy. You can be confident that they will survive the winter and will be less likely to become infested with pests. Ask for recommended roses at a specialist nursery.

8 How can I make sure my roses survive the winter well?

Heaping up soil around the roses protects them from the cold. All underground plant parts are thus made safe from frost. Additional cover supplied by covering up with conifer branches prevents drying out through the action of wind and sun. Young standard roses can be bent down and anchored to the ground, the crown covered with soil and the stem protected with brushwood. (See also pp. 38-43.)

Roses with campanula.

Roses with lady's mantle.

Roses with Michaelmas daisies.

9 How can I avoid disease?

The right choice of position, adequate working of the soil and the purchase of resistant varieties are the main points. In addition, provide space in your garden for useful insects etc., fortify your roses and build up their resistance by using washes and fermented brews and use balanced fertilizing. Form plant communities; for example, with tagetes, marigolds and lavender. (See also pp. 46-55.)

10 What can I do about black spot?

All the preventive measures mentioned in 9 above should be carried out. Plant fortifying brews should be used regularly. Their silicic acid content will stabilise the roses against black spot. If infestation begins, use environmentally friendly fungicides several times in succession. (See also pp. 48 and 51.)

Index

Author's notes

This volume is concerned with the care of roses in the garden. Always wear gloves when handling roses so that you do not injure yourself on the thorns. Store all tools in such a way that no one can injure themselves on them. After use, always clean them immediately before you put them away. If you receive an open wound when working in the garden or when handling soil, you should consult your doctor immediately. In some cases, a tetanus vaccination may be necessary.

Always follow the manufacturer's instructions when using plant protection agents and fertilizers. Keep children and domestic pets away when using them. Also follow all the instructions with respect to handling plant protection agents on page 51. Store plant protection agents and fertilizers in such a way that they are inaccessible to children and domestic pets.

The photographers

The photos in this volume are by Jürgen Becker, with the exception of: Henseler: p. 48 top centre, top right, bottom, 52 top left; mein schoner Garten/Lehmann: Schafer: p. 49 top centre left, bottom right, 52 top right, 53 top centre left; Schneiders, U: p. 41, 44/45, 62/63; Zunke: p. 48 top left, 49 top left, top centre right, top right, bottom left, 52 top centre, bottom, 53 top left, top centre right, top right, bottom.

Acknowledgements

The author would like to thank Swiss "Father of Roses" D. Woesser who taught him much about this wonderful plant.
The photographer Jürgen Becker and the publishers would like to thank the relevant people for their kind help when photographing the following gardens:
Garten Ghyczy/Beesel/Holland (p. 1); Garten Pfordte/Cloppenburg/Germany (p. 4); Garten Dunow/Ratingen/ Germany (p. 17); Rosarium Westfalenpark/Dortmund/Germany (p. 28); Garten Hoffmann/Dortmund Germany (p. 33).

Cover photographs

Front cover: *Shrub rose 'Elmshorn', Rosa 'Class Act', Rosa 'Albertine' type: rambler, Rosa 'Golden Gloves'.* Inside front cover: *A rose-framed entrance with "New Dawn", "Chaplin's Pink Climber" and "Paul Transon".*
Back cover: *Rosa 'Wedding Bells'.*

Reprinted 1998.

This edition published 1996 by Merehurst Limited.
Ferry House, 51-57 Lacy Road, Putney, London SW15 1PR

© 1995 Gräfe und Unzer GmbH, Munich

ISBN 1 85391 564 5

English text copyright © Merehurst Limited 1996
Translated by Astrid Mick
Edited by Lesley Young
Design and typesetting by Paul Cooper Design
Printed in Hong Kong by Wing King Tong

An enchanted garden

Nothing restricts the imagination here. In any garden, no matter whether it is large or small, natural or more formally designed, you can use colours and shapes to your heart's content. Roses offer endless possibilities. They will flower on arches, pergolas and espaliers, grow rampant over fences, climb into trees, cover the ground or create effective features. Roses help to give structure to a garden. They can be used to design fascinating corners, snug places to sit, even geometric patterns. They can hide corners, lead you along paths or mark boundaries. Their charm can also be enhanced by using attractive companion plants.

Climbing rose "Félicité et Perpétué" has completely enveloped this old tree stump with its rosette-like double flowers. It flowers once a year and releases an alluring scent.